10

# C. R. WYLIE Jr.

*William R. Kenan, Jr., Professor of Mathematics, Emeritus*
*Furman University*

# PUZZLES
# IN THOUGHT
# AND LOGIC

Dover Publications Inc., New York

*101 Puzzles in Thought and Logic* is an original work, first published by Dover Publications, Inc., in 1957.

*Standard Book Number: 486-20367-0*
*Library of Congress Catalog Card Number: 57-13026*

Manufactured in the United States of America
Dover Publications, Inc.
31 East 2nd Street
Mineola, N.Y. 11501

# INTRODUCTION

Although life is the greatest puzzle of all, these puzzles are not taken from life, and any resemblance they may bear to actual persons or places is entirely coincidental.

# INTRODUCTION

Puzzles of a purely logical nature are distinguished from riddles, on the one hand, by the fact that they involve no play on words, no deliberately deceptive statements, no guessing — in short, no "catches" of any kind. They differ from quizzes and most mathematical puzzles, on the other hand, in that thought rather than memory, that is, native mental ingenuity rather than a store of acquired information, is the key to their solution.

In order that the puzzles in this collection should conform as nearly as possible to this ideal, every effort has been made to keep the factual basis of each as meager as possible. In a very few instances the use of a little elementary algebra may simplify the solution, but none actually requires any technical information beyond the multiplication tables and the fact that

$$\text{distance} = \text{speed} \times \text{time}$$

It is expected, however, that the reader will recognize that a man must be older than his children, that when two people win a mixed doubles match one is male and the other is female, and a few other equally simple facts from everyday experience.

It is interesting to observe that puzzles of the purely logical type epitomize the entire scientific process. At the outset one is confronted with a mass of more or less unrelated data. From these facts a few positive inferences can perhaps be drawn immediately, but usually it is necessary to set up tentative or working hypotheses to guide the search for a solution. The validity of these hypotheses must then be carefully checked by testing their consequences for consistency with the original data. If inconsistencies appear, the tentative assumptions must be rejected and others substituted until finally a consistent set of conclusions emerges. These conclusions must then be tested for uniqueness to determine whether they alone meet the conditions of the problem or whether there are others equally acceptable.

Thus by repetitions of the fundamental process of setting up an hypothesis, drawing conclusions from it, and examining their consistency within the total framework of the problem, the answer is ultimately wrested from the seemingly incoherent information initially provided. And so it is in science, too.

It is inherent in the nature of logical puzzles that their solution cannot be reduced to a fixed pattern. Nevertheless it may be helpful at this point to offer some general suggestions on how to attack puzzles of this sort. Consider first the following example:

> Boronoff, Pavlow, Revitsky, and Sukarek are four talented creative artists, one a dancer, one a painter, one a singer, and one a writer (though not necessarily respectively).

(1) Boronoff and Revitsky were in the audience the night the singer made his debut on the concert stage.

(2) Both Pavlow and the writer have sat for portraits by the painter.

(3) The writer, whose biography of Sukarek was a best-seller, is planning to write a biography of Boronoff.

(4) Boronoff has never heard of Revitsky.

## What is each man's artistic field?

To keep track mentally of this many facts and the hypotheses and conclusions based upon them is confusing and difficult. In all but the simplest puzzles it is far better to reduce the analysis systematically to a series of written memoranda.

One method of accomplishing this is to set up an array in which all possibilities are encompassed, thus:

|  | dancer | painter | singer | writer |
|---|---|---|---|---|
| Boronoff | | | | |
| Pavlow | | | | |
| Revitsky | | | | |
| Sukarek | | | | |

Now if we consider, for example, that Pavlow cannot be the dancer we will place an X, say, opposite his name in the column headed *dancer*. Or if we decide that Boronoff must be the painter we will place a different mark, say an O, opposite his name in this column, whereupon we can fill the remaining squares in this row and column with X's (since there is only one Boronoff and only one painter). Clearly the solution will be complete when we succeed in placing consistently exactly one O in each row and in each column, thereby showing just what each man is.

In the present problem we know from (1) that neither Boronoff nor Revitsky is the singer, hence we place X's opposite their names in the appropriate column. From (2) we know that Pavlow is neither the painter nor the writer, and from (3) we see that the writer is neither Boronoff nor Sukarek. With the corresponding X's duly entered, the array looks like this:

|  | dancer | painter | singer | writer |
|---|---|---|---|---|
| Boronoff | | | X | X |
| Pavlow | | X | | X |
| Revitsky | | | X | |
| Sukarek | | | | X |

## Introduction

By elimination it is now clear that Revitsky is the writer. Hence we enter an O opposite his name in the column headed *writer* and fill the remaining squares in his row with X's. Moreover, according to (2), Revitsky has sat for the painter, while according to (4) Boronoff does not know Revitsky. Hence Boronoff is not the painter, and so by elimination he must be the dancer. But then neither Pavlow nor Sukarek can be the dancer, and this observation leaves *singer* as the only category possible for Pavlow. Finally, Sukarek must be the painter, and the solution is complete.

The procedure we have just illustrated is also convenient in identification-puzzles where the necessary information is given in the form of conditional or contingent statements. Here is a simple example:

(1) If A is P, C is not R.

(2) If B is P or R, A is Q.

(3) If A is Q or R, B is P.

*Determine the correspondence between the symbols* $(A, B, C)$ *and the symbols* $(P, Q, R)$.

Suppose we begin by accepting the hypothesis "A is P". We then construct an array in which an O appears opposite A in the column headed P and X's appear in the other squares in the A-row and the P-column:

|   | P | Q | R |
|---|---|---|---|
| A | O | X | X |
| B | X |   |   |
| C | X |   |   |

Now from (1), C cannot be R. Hence it must be Q, and necessarily then B must be R. But from (2), if B is R, A must be Q, which contradicts both the assumption that A is P and the conclusion that C is Q. This inconsistency forces us to abandon the hypothesis that A is P.

We continue now by constructing a new array based upon the fact that A is not P. According to (3), if A is not P then B must be P. Hence an O can be entered opposite B in the P-column, and the remaining squares in this row and column can be filled with X's:

|   | P | Q | R |
|---|---|---|---|
| A | X |   |   |
| B | O | X | X |
| C | X |   |   |

Then from (2) we conclude that A is Q, whereupon it follows that C is R, and the solution is complete.

In some puzzles the given information consists of a set of statements, a certain number of which are known to be false without the untrue assertions being identified. Puzzles of this sort can also be conveniently handled through the use of arrays. As an illustration consider the following example:

Shorty Finelli was found shot to death one morning, and the police with better than average luck had three red-hot suspects behind bars by nightfall. That evening the men were questioned and made the following statements.

Buck:  (1) I didn't do it.
(2) I never saw Joey before.
(3) Sure, I knew Shorty.

Joey:  (1) I didn't do it.
(2) Buck and Tippy are both pals of mine.
(3) Buck never killed anybody.

Tippy:  (1) I didn't do it.
(2) Buck lied when he said he'd never seen Joey before.
(3) I don't know who did it.

*If one and only one of each man's statements is false, and if one of the three men is actually guilty, who is the murderer?*

## Introduction

Here the appropriate array is the following

|       | 1 | 2 | 3 |
|-------|---|---|---|
| Buck  |   |   |   |
| Joey  |   |   |   |
| Tippy |   |   |   |

and our problem is to enter one F (for *false*) and two T's (for *true*) in each row in a manner consistent with the given statements.

At the outset we can draw the positive inference that Tippy is innocent. For if he committed the crime, then his first and third statements are both false, contrary to the given condition that only one of each man's assertions is untrue. This conclusion can now be recorded as a T opposite *Tippy* in the first column.

We are now left with two alternatives: either (a) Buck is the guilty one, or (b) Joey is the guilty one. If we assume (a), then Buck's first statement is false and Joey's last statement is false. Under the conditions of the problem this means that Buck's second and Joey's second statement must both be true. But this impossible since they are clearly contradictory. Hence we must abandon the assumption that Buck is the murderer. It follows therefore that Joey is the one who killed Shorty, and this can be checked by examining the completed array for the alternative (b):

|       | 1 | 2 | 3 |
|-------|---|---|---|
| Buck  | T | F | T |
| Joey  | F | T | T |
| Tippy | T | T | F |

# Introduction

Puzzles constructed by the coding or suppression of digits in an arithmetical calculation require no more than attention to obvious numerical facts. Here as in puzzles of the foregoing, more verbal types it is also helpful to keep track of clues and conclusions in an orderly, tabular way. To illustrate, let us consider the following example:

In a certain multiplication problem each digit from 0 to 9 was replaced by a different letter, yielding the coded calculation

```
            A L E
            R U M
          -------
          W I N E
        W U W L
      E W W E
      -----------
      E R M P N E
```

## For what number does each letter stand?

To systematize our work we first write in a row the different letters appearing in the problem:

A L E R U M W I N P

Over each letter we will write its numerical equivalent when we discover it. In the columns under the various letters we will record clues and tentative hypotheses, being careful to put all related inferences on the same horizontal line.

In problems of this sort the digits 0 and 1 can often be found, or at least restricted to a very few possibilities, by simple inspection. For instance, 0 can never occur as the leftmost digit of an integer, and when any number is multiplied by zero the result consists exclusively of zeros. Moreover when any number is multiplied by 1 the result is that number itself. In the present problem, however, we can identify 0 by

# Introduction

an even simpler observation. For in the second column from the right, N plus L equals N, with nothing carried over from the column on the right. Hence L must be zero.

In our search for 1 we can eliminate R, U, and M at once, since none of these, as multipliers in the second row, reproduces A L E. Moreover E cannot be 1 since U times E does not yield a product ending in U. At present, however, we have no further clues as to whether 1 is A, I, N, P, or W.

Now the partial product W U W L ends in L, which we know to be 0. Hence one of the two letters U and E must be 5. Looking at the units digits of the other partial products, we see that both M × E and R × E are numbers ending in E. A moment's reflection (or a glance at a multiplication table) shows that E must therefore be 5.

But if E is 5, then both R and M must be odd, since an even numbers multiplied by 5 would yield a product ending in 0, which is not the case in either the first or third partial product. Moreover, by similar reasoning it is clear that U is an even number.

At this point it is convenient to return to our array and list under U the various possibilities, namely 2, 4, 6, and 8. Opposite each of these we record the corresponding value of W as read from the partial product W U W L, whose last two digits are now determined since the factor A L E is known to be —05. These values of W are easily seen to be 1, 2, 3, and 4.

From an inspection of the second column from the left we can now deduce the corresponding possibilities for R. As we have already noted, R must be odd; hence its value is twice W plus 1 (the 1 being necessarily carried over from the column on the right). The possible values for R are then 3, 5, 7, and 9, and our array looks like this:

```
        0 5
A L E R U M W I N P
        3 2    1
        5 4    2
        7 6    3
        9 8    4
```

Now in the third column from the left in the example the sum of the digits W, U, and W must be more than 9, since 1 had to be carried over from this column into the column on the left. The values in the first two rows of the array are too low for this, however, hence we can cross out both of these lines.

A further consideration of the sum of the digits W, U, and W in the third column from the left, coupled with the fact that M is known to be odd, shows that in the third row of the array M must be 3 while in the fourth row it must be 7. This permits us to reject the third row of the array also, for it contains 3 for both M and W, which is impossible. The correct solution must therefore be the one contained in the fourth row. Hence R is 9, U is 8, M is 7, and W is 4. Substituting these into the problem it is a simple matter to determine that A is 6, I is 2, N is 3, and P is 1. This completes the solution.

As an example of a puzzle involving the suppression rather than the coding of digits, consider the following:

> In a certain problem in long division every digit except 7 was suppressed, yielding

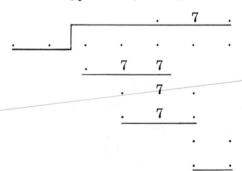

*Restore the missing digits.*

## Introduction

The obvious point of attack here is the first partial product, —77, since it is the most nearly determined number in the problem. Now, the only one-digit numbers whose product ends in 7 are 3 and 9. Hence the first digit in the quotient must be one of these numbers and the last digit in the divisor must be the other. If we consider the possible divisors of the form —9 and multiply each by 3, we find that the only one which yields a product of the form —77 is 59 which gives 177. Alternatively, if we try divisors of the form —3 and multiply each by 9 we find that only 53 yields a product of the form —77. We must reject the first of these two possibilities, however, since when 59 is multiplied by the second digit in the quotient, namely 7, the result is 413, whereas according to the problem the second partial product is of the form —7—. This leaves 53 as the unique possibility for the divisor and 9 as the first digit of the quotient. Finally we observe that the last digit of the quotient must be 1 since the last partial product contains just two digits. Knowing that the divisor is 53 and the quotient is 971, we can multiply these numbers to obtain the dividend. The rest of the problem can then be reconstructed at once.

Most of the puzzles in this collection have unique solutions. A few lead to several different solutions, a circumstance always indicated in the statement of the problem. There are also a few puzzles in which the object is not to find an answer but to prove that there is none, that is to show that the given data, taken all together, are incompatible. As an illustration of a puzzle of this type, consider the following coded subtraction:

```
  E I G H T
− T H R E E
  ─────────
    F I V E
```

*If each letter is supposed to stand for a different digit, prove that there is no possible way to assign a unique digit to each letter to form a correct subtraction.*

We notice first that in the leftmost column the subtraction of T from E leaves 0. Hence E must be exactly 1 more than

T (the 1 having been borrowed from E for use in the second column). Now in the rightmost column, T minus E yields E. (Since E is greater than T, 1 had to be borrowed from the column on the left to make this subtraction possible.) Or to put it in the reverse sense, E plus E is a two-digit number having T in the units place. Hence T must be even, and of course different from 0 since it appears as the leftmost digit in the second row of the problem. We therefore have the following possibilities:

$$\text{T:} \quad 2 \quad 4 \quad 6 \quad 8$$
$$\text{E:} \quad 6 \quad 7 \quad 8 \quad 9$$

Among these there is only one pair, namely E $= 9$, T $= 8$, which meets the further requirement that E is 1 more than T.

Now consider the subtraction in the second column from the right. We have already observed that 1 had to be borrowed from the H for use in the column on the right. Hence E, that is 9, taken away from 1 less than H leaves V. But first borrowing 1 from a number and then taking 9 away from what remains is clearly just the same as taking 10 away from the original number. And when 10 is subtracted from any number, the units digit of the number necessarily appears unchanged as the units digit of the answer. Hence the result of the subtraction in the second column from the right must be H and cannot be the different digit V. This inescapable contradiction proves that the problem cannot be decoded to produce a correct subtraction.

Many of the puzzles in this book are easy to solve, others are rather difficult. It is likely, however, that one person will find some easy that another will find hard, and vice versa, for methods of analysis differ from individual to individual. Within wide limits the time required to solve a particular problem is of little significance as an indication of a person's ability to reason. For one person may by pure chance select the correct assumption for his first trial, while an equally alert individual may unluckily explore any number of fruitless hypotheses before he reaches the right one.

## Introduction

The puzzles herein are all new in substance, though not in form, for a puzzle of an entirely new form is almost unimaginable. None has been published elsewhere. All have been carefully checked and each, whatever its other merits or faults, has been formulated so as to be solvable by logical reasoning with only the barest minimum of acquired information.

And now—pleasant puzzling!

C. R. Wylie Jr.

*Salt Lake City, Utah*

# PUZZLES

**Solutions in back of the book.**

# 1

In a certain bank the positions of cashier, manager, and teller are held by Brown, Jones and Smith, though not necessarily respectively.

> The teller, who was an only child, earns the least.
> Smith, who married Brown's sister, earns more than the manager.

*What position does each man fill?*

# 2

Clark, Daw and Fuller make their living as carpenter, painter and plumber, though not necessarliy respectively.

> The painter recently tried to get the carpenter to do some work for him, but was told that the carpenter was out doing some remodeling for the plumber.
> The plumber makes more money than the painter.
> Daw makes more money than Clark.
> Fuller has never heard of Daw.

*What is each man's occupation?*

# 3

Dorothy, Jean, Virginia, Bill, Jim, and Tom are six young persons who have been close friends from their childhood. They went through high school and college together, and when they finally paired off and became engaged nothing would do but a triple announcement party. Naturally they wanted to break the news to their friends in an unusual fashion, and after some thought they decided upon this scheme.

At just the right moment during the party everyone was given a card bearing the cryptic information:

> Who now are six will soon be three,
> And gaily we confess it,
> But how we've chosen you may know
> No sooner than you guess it.

Tom, who is older than Jim, is Dorothy's brother.
Virginia is the oldest girl.
The total age of each couple-to-be is the same although no two of us are the same age.
Jim and Jean are together as old as Bill and Dorothy.

*What three engagements were announced at the party?*

# 4

Mr. Carter, Mr. Flynn, Mr. Milne, and Mr. Savage serve the little town of Milford as architect, banker, druggist, and grocer, though not necessarily respectively. Each man's income is a whole number of dollars.

The druggist earns exactly twice as much as the grocer, the architect earns exactly twice as much as the druggist, and the banker earns exactly twice as much as the architect.

Although Mr. Carter is older than anyone who makes more money than Mr. Flynn, Mr. Flynn does not make twice as much as Mr. Carter.

Mr. Savage earns exactly $3776 more than Mr. Milne.

*What is each man's occupation?*

arch.          bank          drug.          grocer

C

F

M

S

grocer = x
druggist = 2x
arch. = 4x
banker = 8x

O          2x

F + 2xC

# 5

Brown, Clark, Jones, and Smith are the names of the men who hold, though not necessarily respectively, the positions of accountant, cashier, manager, and president in the First National Bank of Fairport.

Although the cashier beats him consistently, the president will play chess with no one else in the bank.

Both the manager and the cashier are better chess players than the accountant.

Jones and Smith are nextdoor neighbors and frequently play chess together in the evening.

Clark plays a better game of chess than Jones.

The accountant lives near the president but not near any of the others.

*What position does each man hold?*

# 6

Clark, Jones, Morgan, and Smith are four men whose occupation are butcher, druggist, grocer, and policeman, though not necessarily respectively.

Clark and Jones are neighbors and take turns driving each other to work.

Jones makes more money than Morgan.

Clark beats Smith regularly at bowling.

The butcher always walks to work.

The policeman does not not live near the druggist.

The only time the grocer and the policeman ever met was when the policeman arrested the grocer for speeding.

The policeman makes more money than the druggist or the grocer.

*What is each man's occupation?*

# 7

Brown, Clark, Jones and Smith are four substantial citizens who serve their community as architect, banker, doctor, and lawyer, though not necessarily respectively.

Brown, who is more conservative than Jones but more liberal than Smith, is a better golfer than the men who are younger than he is and has a larger income than the men who are older than Clark.

The banker, who earns more than the architect, is neither the youngest nor the oldest.

The doctor, who is a poorer golfer than the lawyer, is less conservative than the architect.

As might be expected, the oldest man is the most conservative and has the largest income, and the youngest man is the best golfer.

*What is each man's profession?*

# 8

In a certain department store the position of buyer, cashier, clerk, floorwalker, and manager are held, though not necessarily respectively, by Miss Ames, Miss Brown, Mr. Conroy, Mr. Davis, and Mr. Evans.

The cashier and the manager were roommates in college.

The buyer is a bachelor.

Evans and Miss Ames have had only business contacts with each other.

Mrs. Conroy was greatly disappointed when her husband told her that the manager had refused to give him a raise.

Davis is going to be the best man when the clerk and the cashier are married.

*What position does each person hold?*

# 9

The positions of buyer, cashier, clerk, floorwalker, and manager in the Empire Department Store are held by Messrs. Allen, Bennett, Clark, Davis, and Ewing.

> The cashier and the floorwalker eat lunch from 11:30 to 12:30, the others eat from 12:30 to 1:30.
> Mrs. Allen and Mrs. Clark are sisters.
> Allen and Bennett always bring their lunch and play cribbage during their lunch hour.
> Davis and Ewing have nothing to do with each other since the day Davis, returning from lunch earlier than usual, found Ewing already gone and reported him to the manager.
> The cashier and the clerk share bachelor quarters.

*What position does each man fill?*

# 10

Jane, Janice, Jack, Jasper, and Jim are the names of five high school chums. Their last names in one order or another are Carter, Carver, Clark, Clayton, and Cramer.

Jasper's mother is dead.

In deference to a certain very wealthy aunt, Mr. and Mrs. Clayton agreed when they were first married that if they ever had a daughter they would name her Janice.

Jane's father and mother have never met Jack's parents.

The Cramer and Carter children have been teammates on several of the school's athletic teams.

When he heard that Carver was going to be out of town on the night of the school's Father and Son banquet, Cramer called Mrs. Carver and offered to "adopt" her son for the evening, but Jack's father had already asked him to go.

The Clarks and Carters, who are very good friends, were delighted when their children began dating each other.

*What is the full name of each youngster?*

# 11

The Smith family, which consists of Mr. and Mrs. Smith, their son, Mr. Smith's sister, and Mrs. Smith's father, has for years dominated the community life of Plainsville. At the present time the five members of the family hold among themselves the positions of grocer, lawyer, postmaster, preacher, and teacher in the little town.

> The lawyer and the teacher are not blood relatives.
> The grocer is younger than her sister-in-law but older than the teacher.
> The preacher, who won his letter playing football in college, is older than the postmaster.

*What position does each member of the family hold?*

# 12

In the Stillwater High School the economics, English, French, history, Latin, and mathematics classes are taught, though not necessarily respectively, by Mrs. Arthur, Miss Bascomb, Mrs. Conroy, Mr. Duval, Mr. Eggleston, and Mr. Furness.

The mathematics teacher and the Latin teacher were roommates in college.

Eggleston is older than Furness but has not taught as long as the economics teacher.

As students, Mrs. Arthur and Miss Bascomb attended one high school while the others attended a different high school.

Furness is the French teacher's father.

The English teacher is the oldest of the six both in age and in years of service. In fact he had the mathematics teacher and the history teacher in class when they were students in the Stillwater High School.

Mrs. Arthur is older than the Latin teacher.

*What subject does each person teach?*

# 13

A recent murder case centered around the six men, Clayton, Forbes, Graham, Holgate, McFee, and Warren. In one order or another these men were the victim, the murderer, the witness, the policeman, the judge, and the hangman. The facts of the case were simple. The victim had died instantly from the effect of a gunshot wound inflicted at close range. The witness did not see the crime committed, but swore to hearing an altercation followed by a shot. After a lengthy trial the murderer was convicted, sentenced to death, and hanged.

McFee knew both the victim and the murderer.

In court the judge asked Clayton to give his account of the shooting.

Warren was the last of the six to see Forbes alive.

The policeman testified that he picked up Graham near the place where the body was found.

Holgate and Warren never met.

*What role did each man play in this unfortunate melodrama?*

# 14

One fine spring afternoon Bill, Ed, and Tom with their wives, whose names in one order or another are Grace, Helen, and Mary, went out and played eighteen holes of golf together.

Mary, Helen, Grace, and Ed shot 106, 102, 100, and 94 respectively.

Bill and Tom shot a 98 and a 96, but for some time they couldn't tell who had made which since they hadn't put their names on their scorecards.

When the fellows finally identified their cards it turned out that two of the couples had the same total score.

Ed's wife beat Bill's wife.

*What is the name of each man's wife, and what scores did Bill and Tom make?*

# 15

Vernon, Wilson, and Yates are three professional men, one an architect, one a doctor, and one a lawyer, who occupy offices on different floors of the same building. Their secretaries are named, though not necessarily respectively, Miss Ainsley, Miss Barnette, and Miss Coulter.

The lawyer has his office on the ground floor.

Instead of marrying her boss the way secretaries do in stories, Miss Barnette became engaged to Yates and goes out to lunch with him every day.

At noon Miss Ainsley goes upstairs to eat lunch with Wilson's secretary.

Vernon had to send his secretary down to borrow some stamps from the architect's office the other day.

*What is each man's profession, and what is the name of each man's secretary?*

# 16

The crew of a certain train consists of a brakeman, a conductor, an engineer, and a fireman, named in one order or another Art, John, Pete, and Tom.

> John is older than Art.
> The brakeman has no relatives on the crew.
> The engineer and the fireman are brothers.
> John is Pete's nephew.
> The fireman is not the conductor's uncle, and the conductor is not the engineer's uncle.

*What position does each man hold, and how are the men related?*

# 17

Ed, Frank, George, and Harry took their wives to the Country Club dance one Saturday evening not long ago. At one time as a result of exchanging dances Betty was dancing with Ed, Alice was dancing with Carol's husband, Dorothy was dancing with Alice's husband, Frank was dancing with George's wife, and George was dancing with Ed's wife.

*What is the name of each man's wife, and with whom was each man dancing?*

# 18

During the summer in Luncyville the shoe store is closed every Monday, the hardware store is closed every Tuesday, the grocery store is closed every Thursday, and the bank is open only on Monday, Wednesday, and Friday. Everything of course is closed on Sunday. One afternoon Mrs. Abbott, Mrs. Briggs, Mrs. Culver, and Mrs. Denny went shopping together, each with a different place to go. On their way they dropped the following remarks:

Mrs. Abbott: Mrs. Denny and I wanted to go earlier in the week but there wasn't a day when we could both take care of our errands.

Mrs. Briggs  I didn't want to come today but tomorrow I couldn't do what I have to do.

Mrs. Culver: I could have gone yesterday or the day before just as well as today.

Mrs. Denny: Either yesterday or tomorrow would have suited me.

*Which place did each woman need to visit in town?*

# 19

Allen, Brady, McCoy, and Smith are the names of four men who have offices on different floors of the same eighteen story building. One of the men is an accountant, one an architect, one a dentist, and one a lawyer.

Allen's office is on a higher floor than McCoy's, although it is lower than Smith's.

Brady's office is below the dentist's.

Smith's office is five times as high as the lawyer's office.

If the architect were to move up two floors he would be halfway between the dentist and the accountant, and if he were to move his office halfway down he would then be midway between the floors where the offices of the dentist and the lawyer are located.

In this particular building the groundfloor is devoted to shops of various kinds and contains no office space. Hence as far as the offices in the building are concerned the first floor is the one immediately above the groundfloor.

*What is each man's profession, and on which floor is each man's office located?*

# 20

Four men, one a famous historian, another a poet, the third a novelist, and the fourth a playwright, named, though not necessarily respectively, Adams, Brown, Clark, and Davis, once found themselves seated together in a pullman car. Happening to look up simultaneously from their reading, they discovered that each was occupied with a book by one of the others. Adams and Brown had just a few minutes before finished the books they had brought and had exchanged with each other. The poet was reading a play. The novelist, who was a very young man with only one book to his credit, boasted that he had never so much as opened a book of history in his life. Brown had brought one of Davis' books, and none of the others had brought one of his own books either

*What was each man reading, and what was each man's literary field?*

# 21

Four black cows and three brown cows give as much milk in five days as three black cows and five brown cows give in four days.

*Which kind of cow is the better milker, black or brown?*

# 22

During a call that I once paid young Mrs. Addlepate I was introduced to her three charming children. By way of making conversation I inquired their ages.

"I can't remember exactly", my hostess replied with a smile, "I'm no good at figures. But if Bill isn't the youngest then I guess Alice is, and if Carl isn't the youngest then Alice is the oldest. Does that help?"

I said that of course it did, although it really didn't at all until days later when it suddenly dawned on me that although Mrs. Addlepate hadn't been able to tell me the ages of her children I could at least tell from her curious remarks which one was the oldest, the next oldest, and the youngest.

*What were the relative ages of the three children?*

# 23

If Tom is twice as old as Howard will be when Jack is as old as Tom is now,

*Who is the oldest, the next oldest, and the youngest?*

# 24

Al, Dick, Jack and Tom were counting up the results of a day's fishing:

Tom had caught more than Jack.
Between them, Al and Dick had caught just as many as Jack and Tom.
Al and Tom had not caught as many as Dick and Jack.

*Who had caught the most, second most, third most, and least?*

# 25

Bill, Hank, Joe, and Tom were amusing themselves one day by playing tug-of-war. Although it was hard, Hank could just outpull Bill and Joe together. Hank and Bill together could just hold Tom and Joe, neither pair being able to budge the other. However if Joe and Bill changed places, then Tom and Bill won rather easily.

*Of the four fellows, who was the strongest, next strongest, and so on?*

# 26

Bowman, Crawford, Jennings, and Stewart are four members of the Mountain View Golf Club. Their ages are all different and so are their golfing abilities, but nevertheless they make an inseparable foursome. One day as they teed off on the first hole a new member of the club who had seen them play together several times turned to his companion on the terrace and asked who they were and how their games compared.

"I don't know exactly", his companion replied, "but I guess it's correct to say that although Jennings is a better golfer than anyone of the four who is older than Crawford, and although anyone of the four who can beat Stewart is at least as old as Bowman, the best golfer, while younger than anyone Stewart can beat, is not the youngest, and while at least as old as anyone Bowman can beat, is not the oldest".

"I see", said the new member politely, inwardly convinced that as far as this information was concerned, the only way he'd ever be able to rank the four would be to play them himself.

However from the facts given it is possible to determine unambigously just who is the best golfer, who is the second best, and so on.

*Can you?*

# 27

Alice, Grace, Helen, and Mary were discussing their ages during a recent bridge game. Each knew perfectly well how old her companions were, but nevertheless they discussed the matter, as adults are apt to do, with that indirection and circumlocution which the mature mind invariably confuses with actual secrecy. To prove that this is neither an empty witticism nor an unwarranted slander, here are four facts disclosed by the young women during the more obscure part of their conversation, and I leave it to anyone to determine in sixty seconds or less not only the relative ages of the four but also how they were paired during this portion of their game.

Mary is younger than Grace.
Helen is older than either of her opponents.
Mary is older than her partner.
Alice and Grace are together older than Helen and Mary.

# 28

Among one hundred applicants for a certain technical position it was discovered that ten had never taken a course in chemistry or in physics. Seventy-five had taken at least one course in chemistry. Eighty-three had taken at least one course in physics.

*How many of the applicants had had some work in both chemistry and physics?*

# 29

The following is a portion of a report submitted by an investigator for a well-known market analysis agency with standards of accuracy so high that it boasts that an employee's first mistake is his last.

| | |
|---|---:|
| Number of consumers interviewed _____ | 100 |
| Number who drink coffee _____ | 78 |
| Number who drink tea _____ | 71 |
| Number who drink both tea and coffee _____ | 48 |

*Why was the interviewer discharged?*

# 30

A census taker, reporting on a certain community consisting exclusively of young married couples and their children, stated that

There were more parents than there were children.
Every boy had a sister.
There were more boys than girls.
There were no childless couples.

*Why was he reprimanded and his report rejected?*

# 31

Mr. and Mrs. O. Howe Fruitful were well blessed with children, so that the difficulties usually confronting parents were for them almost insurmountable. For instance, of their ample brood seven wouldn't touch spinach, six wouldn't eat carrots, and five wouldn't eat beans. Four would eat neither spinach nor carrots, three would eat neither spinach nor beans, and two would touch neither carrots nor beans. One of the children wouldn't eat spinach, carrots, or beans. And none would eat all three of the vegetables.

*How many children were there in the family?*

# 32

In a certain apartment house occupied exclusively by young married couples and their children the following facts are known to be true.

There are more children than adults, more adults than boys, more boys than girls, and more girls than families.

There are no childless couples, and no two families have the same number of children.

Every girl has at least one brother and at most one sister.

One family has more children than all the others put together.

*How many families are there, and how many boys and girls are there in each family?*

# 33

One afternoon Mrs. Marshall, Mrs. Price, Mrs. Torrey, and Mrs. Winters went shopping together, each with two errands to perform. One of the women had to visit the hardware store, two needed to go to the bank, two needed to go to the butcher shop, and all but one needed to buy groceries. Their shopping was simplified quite a bit by the fact they lived in a small town which had only one store of each kind and only one bank. As a result they were soon done and on their way home. If

> Doris didn't go into the grocery store,
> Both Ethel and Mrs. Winters bought meat,
> Margaret came home with more money than she had when she started,
> Mrs. Price didn't go into any of the places where Lucille or Mrs. Torrey went,

*What was each woman's full name, and what two places did each visit?*

# 34

In a certain small high school the courses in biology, economics, English, French, history, and mathematics are taught by just three men, Mitchell, Morgan, and Myers, each of whom teaches two subjects.

The economics teacher and the French teacher are next-door neighbors.

Mitchell is the youngest of the three.

The men ride to and from school together, Myers, the biology teacher, and the French teacher each driving one week out of three.

The biology teacher is older than the mathematics teacher.

When they can find a fourth, the English teacher, the mathematics teacher, and Mitchell usually spend their lunch hour playing bridge.

*What subjects does each man teach?*

# 35

In one of the famous resort towns of Europe, where tourists from a dozen countries may always be encountered, four travelers once struck up an acquaintance. They were of different nationalities and although each man could speak two of the four languages, English, French, German, and Italian, there was still no common tongue in which they could all converse. In fact only one of the languages was spoken by more than two of the men.

Nobody spoke both French and German.

Although John couldn't speak English he could still act as interpreter when Peter and Jacob wanted to speak to each other.

Jacob spoke German and could also talk to William although the latter knew not a word of German.

John, Peter, and William could not all converse in the same language.

*What two languages did each man speak?*

# 36

A group of men discussing their fraternal affiliations found the following curious facts to be true:

> Each man belonged to exactly two lodges.
> Each lodge was represented in the group by exactly three men.
> Every possible pair of lodges had exactly one member of the group in common.

*How many men were there in the group, and how many different lodges were represented?*

# 37

The Interfraternity Council at Juke Box Tech presented a highly involved situation last year. Each fraternity was represented by four men according to the rules of the council, but because of overlapping memberships the following complications existed:

> Each man on the council was simultaneously the representative of two different fraternities.
>
> Every pair of fraternities had one representative in common.

In this welter of conflicting allegiances the council accomplished little or nothing, which of course was not unusual. However it did present an interesting puzzle, namely:

*How many fraternities were represented on the council and how many representatives were there altogether?*

# 38

Five men whose given names were Louis, Martin, Norris, Oliver, and Peter, and whose last names in one order or another were Atwood, Bartlett, Campbell, Donovan, and Easterling, although living in the same small town had through the years become more or less estranged until finally the following conditions existed:

Bartlett would only speak to two of the others.

Although Peter would speak to all but one, Louis would only speak to one of the others.

Donovan and Martin wouldn't speak, although Norris and Easterling would.

Martin, Norris, and Oliver were all on speaking terms.

There was only one of the five that Atwood wouldn't speak to, and only one of the five to whom Campbell would speak.

*What was each man's full name, and to whom would each man speak?*

# 39

Six men, Andrews, Blaine, Colter, Doister, Ebert, and Fisher, are the only members eligible for the offices of president, vice-president, and secretary in a certain organization. If

> Andrews won't be an officer unless Ebert is president,
> Blaine won't serve if he outranks Colter,
> Blaine won't serve with Fisher under any conditions,
> Colter won't serve with both Ebert and Fisher,
> Colter won't serve if Fisher is president or Blaine is secretary,
> Doister won't serve with Colter or Ebert unless he outranks them,
> Ebert won't be vice-president,
> Ebert won't be secretary if Doister is an officer,
> Ebert won't serve with Andrews unless Fisher serves too,
> Fisher won't serve unless either he or Colter is president,

*How can the three offices be filled?*

# 40

The nominating committee of the All Friends Club recently had to present a slate of candidates for the offices of president, vice-president, secretary, and treasurer. Those eligible were Arthur, Burton, Congreve, Downs, Ewald, and Flynn. The lot of any nominating committee is difficult, but this one found its task almost impossible, for

> Arthur wouldn't serve unless Burton did too, and even then he wouldn't be vice-president,
> Burton wouldn't serve as vice-president or as secretary,
> Congreve wouldn't serve with Burton unless Flynn served too,
> Downs wouldn't serve with Ewald or Flynn under any circumstances,
> Ewald wouldn't serve with both Arthur and Burton,
> Flynn wouldn't serve except as president, and he wouldn't do that if Congreve was vice-president.

*What slate of candidates did the committee finally present?*

# 41

In a certain organization there are eight men eligible to serve on a newly established committee of four. The selection of the members is not an easy matter, however, for there are jealousies and attachments among the candidates which prevent a free choice of four committeemen. If you were the president of the organization could you select a committee of four satisfying all these whims?

Ames will serve with anybody.

Brown won't serve unless Clayton serves.

Clayton won't serve with Evans.

Davis won't serve without Hughes.

Evans will serve with anybody.

French won't serve with Davis unless Grant serves too, and won't serve with Clayton unless Davis also serves.

Grant won't serve with both Brown and Clayton, and won't serve with either Ames or Evans.

Hughes won't serve unless either Brown or French serves and won't serve with Clayton unless Grant serves too, and won't serve with both Ames and Evans.

# 42

The personnel director of a firm in speaking of three men the company was thinking of hiring once said,

"We need Brown and if we need Jones then we need Smith, if and only if we need either Brown or Jones and don't need Smith."

*If the company actually needed more than one of the men, which ones were they?*

# 43

Bertrand Russell in a whimsical moment once defined mathematics as " . . . the subject in which we never know what we are talking about, nor whether what we are saying is true," and here is a puzzle of which the same thing might be said.

As a simple exercise in abstraction suppose that four meaningless symbols *A*, *B*, *C*, and *D* correspond in one order or another to the equally meaningless symbols *W*, *X*, *Y*, and *Z*, and suppose further that

> If *A* is not *X*, then *C* is not *Y*.
> If *B* is either *Y* or *Z*, then *A* is *X*.
> If *C* is not *W*, then *B* is *Z*.
> If *D* is *Y*, then *B* is not *X*.
> If *D* is not *X*, then *B* is *X*.

*In what order do the two sets of symbols correspond?*

# 44

Three men named Barber, Cutler, and Drake have wives named Beth, Dorothy, and Louise. Each couple has a son, the names of the boys being Allan, Henry and Victor.

Drake is neither Louise's husband nor Henry's father.

Beth is neither Cutler's wife nor Allan's mother.

If Allan's father is either Cutler or Drake, then Louise is Victor's mother.

If Louise is Cutler's wife, Dorothy is not Allan's mother.

*What is the name of each man's wife and son?*

# 45

Three men named Lewis, Miller, and Nelson fill the positions of accountant, cashier, and clerk in the leading department store in Centerburg.

If Nelson is the cashier, Miller is the clerk.

If Nelson is the clerk, Miller is the accountant.

If Miller is not the cashier, Lewis is the clerk.

If Lewis is the accountant, Nelson is the clerk.

*What is each man's job?*

# 46

Dick's work in mathematics had been on the borderline between $A$ and $B$ during most of the term, so one day just before examinations he stayed after class to ask his teacher what final grade he might reasonably expect. With Dick were two of his pals who had the same question in mind.

"Well," said the teacher to Dick, "if you get an $A$ then I'll either have to give Henry a $C$ or John a $B$. But if John doesn't get a $B$ then either you won't get an $A$ or Henry won't get a $C$. On the other hand, though, if John gets a $B$ and Henry doesn't get a $C$ then you won't get an $A$. Is that clear?"

The boys thanked their teacher and left, not a bit the wiser but determined to study diligently to the end of the term.

*Now the question is this, if John and Henry received the same final grade, did Dick get his A?*

# 47

Long ago in a forgotten country of the east there existed a remarkable oracle. Unlike most oracles it was not the mouthpiece of a single deity but of three, the God of Truth, the God of Falsehood, and the God of Diplomacy. These gods were represented by three identical figures seated in a row behind the altar at which their petitioners knelt. The gods were always ready to answer their mortal supplicants, but since their identities were impossible to determine because their images were exactly alike, no one ever knew whether the reply to his question came from the God of Truth and hence could be relied on, or whether it came from the God of Falsehood and so was certainly untrue, or whether it came from the God of Diplomacy and hence might be either true or false. This confusion of course did not deter the multitudes from seeking advice, though it did create a very profitable sideline for the priests of the temple who, for a price, were always ready to interpret the utterances of the oracle.

One day a sacrilegious fool came to the altar vowing to do what the wisest men of the past had failed to accomplish, namely to expose the identity of each god.

Said he to the figure on the left, "Who sittest next to thee?"

"The God of Truth," was the answer.

Then said the fool to the image in the center, "Who art thou?"

"The God of Diplomacy," was the answer.

Lastly to the image on the right the fool said, "Who sittest next to thee?"

"The God of Falsehood," came the reply.

"Oho," said the fool to himself, "so that's the way of it."

And straightway he established an interpreting concession just outside the temple and soon had driven the priests out of business through the uncanny accuracy of his interpretations.

*Can you, like the fool in the legend, determine the identity of each god from the answers they made to the three simple questions they were asked?*

# 48

Just before the end of the term four high school students were discussing their chances for certain grades. The following remarks contain the gist of their hopes and fears.

| | |
|---|---|
| Jack: | We'll all get different grades. |
| | If I get an *A*, then Lucy will get a *D*. |
| Jean: | If Lucy gets a *C*, then Jack will get a *D*. |
| | Jack will get a better grade than Paul. |
| Lucy: | If Jean doesn't get an *A*, then Jack will get a *C*. |
| | If I get a *B*, then Paul won't get a *D*. |
| Paul: | If Lucy gets an *A*, then I'll get a *B*. |
| | If Jean doesn't get a *B*, I won't either. |

When the final examinations were graded and the term marks made out each of the four passed, and strange as it may seem, each received a grade that checked exactly with all the ideas they had previously expressed.

*What grade did each receive?*

# 49

Four men, one of whom was known to have committed a certain crime, made the following statements when questioned by the police.

Archie: Dave did it.
Dave: Tony did it.
Gus: I didn't do it.
Tony: Dave lied when he said I did it.

*If only one of these four statements is true, who was the guilty man? On the other hand, if only one of these four statements is false, who was the guilty man?*

# 50

Grace, Helen, and Mary were discussing their ages one day, and in the course of their conversation they made the following assertions.

Grace: I am twenty-two.
I am two years younger than Helen.
I am a year older than Mary.

Helen: I am not the youngest.
Mary and I are three years apart.
Mary is twenty-five.

Mary: I am younger than Grace.
Grace is twenty three.
Helen is three years older than Grace.

It is of course too much to expect that three young women should be entirely truthful when speaking of their ages, and in the present instance only two of the three statements made by each girl are true.

*Can you deduce the age of each one?*

# 51

Three men were once arrested for a crime which beyond a shadow of a doubt had been committed by one of them. Preliminary questioning disclosed the curious fact that one of the suspects was a highly respected judge, one just an average citizen, and one a notorious crook. In what follows they will be referred to as Brown, Jones, and Smith, though not necessarily respectively. Each man made two statements to the police, which were in effect

| | |
|---|---|
| Brown: | I didn't do it. |
| | Jones didn't do it. |
| Jones: | Brown didn't do it. |
| | Smith did it. |
| Smith: | I didn't do it. |
| | Brown did it. |

Further investigation showed, as might have been expected, that both statements made by the judge were true, both statements made by the criminal were false, and of the two statements made by the average man one was true and one was false.

*Which of the three men was the judge, the average citizen, the crook? And who committed the crime?*

# 52

Four men were eating dinner together in a restaurant when one of them suddenly struggled to his feet, cried out "I've been poisoned," and fell dead. His companions were arrested on the spot and under questioning made the following statements, exactly one of which is false in each case.

Watts:  I didn't do it.
I was sitting next to O'Neil.
We had our usual waiter today.

Rogers:  I was sitting across the table from Smith.
We had a new waiter today.
The waiter didn't do it.

O'Neil:  Rogers didn't do it.
It was the waiter who poisoned Smith.
Watts lied when he said we had our usual waiter today.

Assuming that only Smith's companions and the waiter are implicated,

*Who was the murderer?*

# 53

In the Plain City High School the classes in chemistry, history, Latin, and mathematics are taught, though not necessarily respectively, by Mr. Ames, Mr. Brown, Miss Clark, and Miss Davis. According to the school's yearbook,

> When they were in college the Latin teacher and the mathematics teacher won first prize in an all-campus tango contest.
> Mrs. Ames is president of the Plain City P.T.A.
> The chemistry teacher and the mathematics teacher were roommates in college.
> The chemistry teacher is also the football coach.
> The history teacher and the Latin teacher are engaged to each other.
> Mr. Ames, Mr. Brown, and Miss Clark went to different colleges.

However, as everyone knows, a high school annual contains a certain amount of school gossip in addition to its factual summary of the year's activities, and hence is not always completely reliable. In the present case exactly five of the statements given are true and one is false.

*What subject does each person teach?*

# 54

Mr. and Mrs. Smith and their two children form a typical American family. According to one of their more talkative neighbors,

> George and Dorothy are blood relatives.
> Howard is older than George.
> Virginia is younger than Howard.
> Virginia is older than Dorothy.

If two and only two of these statements are true,

*What is the first name of each member of the family?*

Mom          Virginia

Dad    ~~George~~    George

Sister    Dorothy    Dorothy

Brother    ~~George~~ George    Howard

# 55

Brown, Jones, and Smith are employed by the City of Plainsfield as fireman, policeman, and teacher, though not necessarily respectively. Plainsfield is a very neighborly little town, and someone once reported that,

> Brown and the teacher are neighbors.
> Jones and the teacher are neighbors.
> Both Brown and Smith are neighbors of the fireman.
> Both the policeman and the fireman are neighbors of Jones.
> The men are all neighbors.

However the truth of the matter is that only two of these statements are true.

*Can you determine the job which each man holds?*

# 56

When Bill, Ed, Jim, and Tom started an eighteen-hole golf match the other day they discovered that no one had brought a pencil, so they had to carry their scores in their heads. As a result they got things a bit mixed up. In fact only two of the four statements made by each player as they tried to determine the winner were correct.

Bill:     I beat Jim and Tom.
             Ed shot 111.
             Jim took 6 on the last hole.
             None of us broke 100.

Ed:       Bill wasn't last.
             I was the winner.
             Jim finally broke 100.
             I shot 98.

Jim:      I beat Bill and Ed.
             The last hole wasn't my best.
             We didn't all break 100.
             Tom wasn't the winner.

Tom:     Ed beat Bill.
             I was the winner.
             Bill placed between Ed and Jim.
             The last hole was Jim's best.

Knowing this, and the fact that all the scores were different,

*Can you tell from the statements they made at the "nineteenth hole" who was first, second, third, and last?*

# 57

Bill Bianchi was shot to death at close range on a lonely country road late one night. The police soon established that the murder was committed by one of four men, Al, Jack, Joe, and Tom, and that the gun that was used belonged to one of the four. Each man was questioned and made the statements listed below, two and only two of which are true in each case.

Al:
I didn't do it.
Tom did it.
Sure I own a gun.
Joe and I were playing poker when Bill was shot.

Jack:
I didn't do it.
Al did it.
Joe and I were at the movies when Bill was shot.
Bill was shot with Joe's gun.

Joe:
I was asleep when Bill was shot.
Al lied when he said Tom killed Bill.
Jack is the only one of us who owns a gun.
Tom and Bill were pals.

Tom:
I never fired a gun in my life.
I don't know who did it.
Joe doesn't own a gun.
I never saw Bill until they showed me the body.

*Who killed Bianchi?*

# 58

Edward, Howard, and John are three high school students each of whom is taking three of the four subjects, biology, chemistry, history, and mathematics. One day while talking about their programs they made the following statements.

Edward: There is just one subject we're all taking.
I'm the only one of us who is taking mathematics.
No two of us are taking the same three subjects.
John is wrong when he says that Howard and I are both taking chemistry.

Howard: Ed is the only one of us who is taking history.
John and I are taking the same subjects.
We're all taking biology.
Two of us are taking both chemistry and biology.

John: We're all taking mathematics.
Howard is taking history.
Ed is taking one subject that I'm not.
Both Howard and Ed are taking chemistry.

If two and only two of each boy's statements are true,

*What subjects is each boy taking?*

# 59

Bill, Jack, and Tom went fishing together one day. Around the campfire that evening, as they elaborated the day's adventure for their wives, their talk took somewhat the following turn.

Bill:   Tom only caught two fish.
        Jack caught one more than Tom.
        Jack and I together caught eight more than
           Tom.
        I caught more than the others put together.
Jack:   Tom caught the most.
        I caught three more than Bill.
        Tom's wrong when he says I didn't catch any.
        Bill and Tom caught the same number.
Tom:    Jack didn't catch any.
        Bill is wrong when he says I only caught two.
        Bill and I didn't catch the same number.
        Between them, Jack and Bill caught thirteen.

The meaning of such obviously contradictory statements as these is entirely obscure until one realizes that try as he will, no confirmed fisherman can tell the truth more than half the time, and these three were no exceptions. In fact just two of the four statements made by each man were true.

## How many fish did each man catch?

# 60

Four men, Adams, Bates, Clark, and Douglas, were speaking of their wives. They were not well acquainted and the statements they made, as listed below, are not all accurate. In fact the only thing which is certain is that each statement in which a man mentions his own wife's name is correct.

Adams:    Dorothy is Jean's mother.
               I have never met Patricia.

Bates:    Clark's wife is either Dorothy or Patricia.
               Jean is the oldest.

Clark:    Patricia is Adams' wife.
               Dorothy is Jean's older sister.

Douglas: Margaret is my daughter.
               Dorothy is older than my wife.

*What is the given name of each man's wife?*

# 61

Four men, Brown, Fairgrieve, Leonard, and Whittier, are each enthusiastic participants in one of the four sports, bowling, fishing, golf, and tennis. At lunch one day their talk turned to athletics, and for some time they discussed their individual interests and activities. Naturally, much of their talk was repetitious, and the gist of their remarks is adequately summarized in the following statements.

Brown: Whittier doesn't like either golf or tennis.
This time last Saturday I was bowling with Fairgrieve.

Fairgrieve: Tennis isn't my favorite sport.
This time last Saturday I was bowling with Leonard.

Leonard: I like fishing better than golf.
This time last Saturday I was playing tennis with Brown.

Whittier: Bowling is Leonard's favorite sport.
Fairgrieve doesn't like either tennis or golf.

If each man has a different favorite sport, and if all that can be guaranteed about their comments is that each statement in which a man mentions his own first choice is necessarily true,

*What is each man's favorite sport?*

# 62

Four men, Brown, Harris, Jones, and Smith, were talking about their sons one day. Among the statements they made were the following, some of which are true, some false, the only thing certain being that each statement in which a man mentions the name of his own son is necessarily correct.

Brown: Al graduates from high school next month.
Carl hasn't had a vacation since he started working two years ago.
Bill's wife can't get him to take any kind of exercise.

Harris: Bill is going to be married next spring.
Dick has been dating my daughter.
Al and Carl played on the freshman football team in college this year.

Jones: Al will be nine tomorrow.
Bill is younger than Al.
Carl and Dick are coming home from a hunting trip today.

Smith: Bill and Jones won the Club's Father and Son Handball Tournament.
Dick told me yesterday that he hadn't seen Carl for a long time.
Al and Carl were roommates in college last year.

*What is the name of each man's son?*

# 63

The little town of Plainview is exactly like hundreds of other inconspicuous country communities in every respect but one. Its scenery, its stores, its churches all have their counterparts at every crossroads in America, but as the home of the Murphy boys the town is unique. These remarkable boys, Bill and John, exhibit, for reasons as yet entirely unknown, a most peculiar aberration with respect to truth and falsehood. Bill is apparently incapable of telling the truth on Monday, Tuesday, or Wednesday, although he invariably does so on the other days of the week. His brother similarly finds it impossible to avoid lying on Tuesday, Thursday, or Saturday, although during the rest of the week it is equally impossible for him not to speak the truth.

When I heard of these unusual youngsters on my recent visit to Plainview I determined to meet them and observe for myself their peculiar behavior. Accordingly I called at their home and found the boys playing in the yard.

"Hello," I said, "what's your name?"

"I'm Bill," replied the older without hesitation.

"What day is it today?" I continued, feeling myself quite the experimental psychologist.

"Well yesterday was Sunday," said the older boy.

"And tomorrow is Friday," his brother added.

"Wait a minute," I said to the latter, "that doesn't sound right. Are you sure you're telling the truth?"

"I always tell the truth on Wednesdays," he replied.

At that moment our conversation was interrupted by the boys' mother. After passing the time of day with her I turned to find the boys gone about their play, and I had no further words with them.

Now to me the most curious thing about the whole episode was that in spite of the dubious reliability of the boys' remarks it was possible, putting them all together, to infer from them with complete certainty the day of the week on which the encounter took place and also the correct name of the older and of the younger boy.

*When did the meeting take place, and what was the name of each boy?*

# 64

Three identical boxes, one containing two black marbles, one containing a black marble and a white one, and the third containing two white marbles, are placed side by side on a table. Originally each box bore a tag describing its content, but somehow the labels got mixed up so that each one was incorrect. Now for some reason or other (if only to make a puzzle) it is desired to determine the contents of each box by a sampling process, that is by choosing one of the boxes, drawing blindly one of the marbles it contains, and repeating this procedure as often as necessary until the contents of each box can be positively inferred.

*What is the most efficient way to sample, in order to identify the contents of each box with the fewest draws?*

# 65

Hank Miller, a small-time gambler and racketeer, was shot and fatally wounded in front of the pool hall in Smalltown by someone driving past in a big sedan. Hank had a number of enemies, but the police soon narrowed down their search for the killer to three men who were apprehended in Bigtown several days after the murder. At the time of their arrest the authorities were morally certain that one of these three was guilty, and subsequent developments proved this to be correct. Each of the men had a lengthy police record and was congenitally incapable of making three consecutive statements without lying. Nevertheless they were questioned, and their assertions are listed here for whatever they may be worth.

Lefty:  Spike killed Hank.
I never was in Smalltown in my life.
I'm innocent.

Spike:  Red is innocent.
Everything Lefty said is a lie.
I didn't do it.

Red:  I didn't kill him.
Lefty lied when he said he'd never been in Smalltown.
Spike lied when he said that everything Lefty said was a lie.

## Who killed Miller?

# 66

Once upon a time an aged king, nearing the end of his days and having no heir to succeed him upon the throne, cast about him for a worthy successor. In all corners of his kingdom he caused search to be made for young men of promise. These he gathered together by districts for further judging and selection, and so again and again until the four most gifted men of country were determined and brought before him for a final choice. So near alike in their capabilities were they that no ordinary test could mark one as superior to his companions, and in order to make his final decision the king devised this scheme.

The four were tightly blindfolded and seated around a table. While seated thus the king said to them, "In a moment I shall touch each of you upon the forehead, and mayhap I shall leave upon you a black mark and mayhap a white mark. I shall then cause your bandages to be removed and each of you who, looking upon his companions, sees more black marks than white marks is to stand and remain erect until such time as one of you can state convincingly the color of the mark he bears. That one I shall name my successor."

According to his word the king touched each man upon the forehead. When the blindfolds were removed each man looked at his fellows and at once arose. For many minutes each stood silent, pondering. Finally one man spoke, saying "Sire, I bear a black mark," and straightway gave convincing argument for his assertion.

*How did the king actually mark the men, and how did the successful candidate prove the existence of a black mark upon his forehead?*

# 67

Four men were once given the following test. Identical boxes, one containing three black balls, one containing two black balls and one white ball, the third containing one black ball and two white balls, and the fourth containing three white balls, were placed before them. Each box bore one of the labels

Three Black

Two Black — One White

One Black — Two White

Three White

but, as the men were told befor : the test began, the four labels had been mixed up so that none described correctly the contents of the box to which it was attached. Each man was assigned one of the boxes, whose label only he was permitted to see. Then 'in ignorance of its contents, except for such dubious information as its incorrect tag might convey, each was to draw blindly two of the three balls from his box and endeavor to tell from them the color of the remaining ball.

The test was not overly difficult, and the first man after drawing his pair announced at once, "I've drawn two black balls, and I can tell what the third ball is."

The second man likewise drew two balls from his box and promptly declared, "I've drawn one white and one black ball, and I know the color of the remaining ball."

The third man was somewhat impatient, and after comparing the balls he had drawn with the label on his box he remarked without further thought. "I've drawn two white balls, but I can't tell what the third one is."

The last man had the hardest job of all, for he was blind and so didn't even know the label his box bore. However he thought for some time and then declared, "I don't need to draw. I know the color of each of the balls in my box, and what's more I know the color of the third ball in each of your boxes too."

The other men were all amazed by the blind man's assertion and immediately challenged him, whereupon he quickly and logically convinced them that he was entirely correct in saying that he knew the contents of every box.

*How did he tell?*

# 68

Mrs. Davis, Mrs. Jones, and Mrs. Smith, whose first names are Dorothy, Helen, and Mary, though not necessarily respectively, went shopping together one day. While downtown, Mary spent twice as much as Helen and Helen spent three times as much as Dorothy. If Mrs. Davis spent $3.85 more than Mrs. Smith,

*What is each woman's full name?*

# 69

Four men whose last names were Conner, Morgan, Smith and Wells, and whose first names were Al, Bill, Jack, and Tom, though not necessarily respectively, amused themselves during their lunch hour one day by playing a game in which the winner of the first game was to collect ten cents from each of the others, the winner of the second game was to collect twenty cents from each of the others, the winner of the third game was to collect thirty cents from each of the others, and so on. The play ended and the men went back to work after four turns, each man having won once, Jack taking the first game, Morgan the second, Bill the third, and Smith the last. In the beginning Tom had the most money, and at the end Wells had the most.

*What was the full name of each of the players?*

# 70

Farmer Brown sent his boy John into town the other day with a load of melons for market.

"Now remember", he said, "these here melons up front are better than those in back, and I want you to sell 'em two for a quarter. The other half you can let go at three for a quarter".

On the way into town John kept thinking, "Half of 'em two for a quarter, half of 'em three for a quarter, ...." until finally he said to himself, "That's too much figurin'. They don't look different enough to tell apart, and I'm agoin' to sell 'em all at ten cents apiece."

Business was good, and John sold all his melons in time to get back to the farm for supper. But when he gave his father the money he'd made, Farmer Brown counted it and then blew up, for it was a dollar short.

"Did you spend any of this money on city foolishness?" said he.

"No, sir," said John.

"Well then, did you sell 'em like I told you, two for a quarter and three for a quarter?"

"Yes and no," said John. "You see I figured that two for a quarter and three for a quarter was the same as five for fifty cents, so I just sold 'em all for ten cents apiece. Ain't that right?"

"You numbskull," was all Farmer Brown would say, as he packed John off to bed without any supper.

*Can you tell how John happened to come out a dollar short on the transaction, and how many melons he sold altogether?*

# 71

A hiker can average two miles per hour uphill and six miles per hour downhill. Going uphill and down, and if he spends no time at the summit,

*What will be his average speed for an entire trip?*

# 72

As the good ship *Pleasure City* steamed out of Lake James, past the town of Bayview, and into the swiftly flowing Wolf River, which empties into the lake at the little resort town after coursing straight as an arrow through a hundred miles of enchanting wilderness, her captain surely could have found in the bright sunlight and moving shadows of the day no hint of the storm that was soon to break. But break it did, for at 12:30 Mrs. Smythe, whose wealth and position had secured to her the leadership of what social life there was among the passengers on the week's excursion, burst into the captain's quarters charging that her jewels had been stolen, and accusing the ship's steward or one of the two maids assigned to her deck. From her story and from the stories told by the three suspects the captain pieced together the following facts.

Beyond question the jewels had been stolen no more than a few hours before their loss was discovered. In attempting to be more explicit Mrs. Smythe recalled that at 10:30 the morning maid came in with coffee which she received in bed. As the maid departed through the adjoining sitting room she was heard rummaging among things there, and on being so charged left hurriedly without reply. This maid admitted returning to make the bed just before she went off duty at 12:00. From 12:10 to 12:20 she was seen washing and changing her clothes in the maid's dressing room. From 12:00 to 12:10 and from 12:20 to 12:30 she could offer no alibi.

The afternoon maid entered the suite promptly at 12:00 to clean. At 12:05 she was interrupted by the steward who, with the two maids, was the only person besides Mrs. Smythe who could possibly have had access to the suite. He told her to leave until he could fix some lightbulbs that needed changing. At 12:10 Mrs. Smythe suddenly returned to her rooms, found the steward apparently snooping among her belongings, and engaged in a lengthy argument with him over the matter. This lasted until 12:25 when the afternoon maid returned to continue her cleaning. At 12:30 Mrs. Smythe missed her jewels and immediately took the matter to the captain, as related above.

Beyond the facts already listed, upon which all parties seemed independently agreed, the only other information of which the captain felt sure was that the robbery was a solo job, and that whichever of the three suspects was guilty, he or she had no accomplice on the ship. Unable to proceed further, the captain at 1:30 gave orders to return to Bayview, intending to place the matter in the hands of the local police. However, at 2:45 a lookout sighted a jar floating in the water, and on retrieving it found it to contain all the jewels. This development completely altered the situation, and when the ship docked at Bayview the captain placed not the problem but its solution in the hands of the police.

*Who was the guilty party, and how did the captain decide the matter?*

# 73

If it takes twice as long for a passenger train to pass a freight train after it first overtakes it as it takes the two trains to pass when going in opposite directions,

*How many times faster than the freight train is the passenger train?*

# 74

A woodsman paddling steadily across the still surface of a northern lake saw a magnificent bass break water directly ahead of him. Twelve strokes he counted until his canoe first crossed the ever-widening circle the fish had made, and then twelve more before he broke through the circle on the opposite side. For a time thereafter he sought relief from the pleasant monotony of his journey by calculating how far away the fish had been at the moment it jumped, but it proved too much for him and he soon gave himself up to less specific thoughts.

*Can you complete his calculation?*

# 75

Both the Allens and the Smiths have two young sons under eleven. The names of the boys, whose ages rounded off to the nearest year are all different, are Arthur, Bert, Carl, and David. Taking the ages of the boys only to the nearest year, the following statements are true.

Arthur is three years younger than his brother.
Bert is the oldest.
Carl is half as old as one of the Allen boys.
David is five years older than the younger Smith boy.
The total ages of the boys in each family differ by the same amount today as they did five years ago.

*How old is each boy, and what is each boy's family name?*

# 76

When Tom and Betty applied for their marriage license the first thing they were asked was their ages. With a natural reluctance to reveal so important a secret Betty said that they were both in their twenties, and wasn't that close enough. The clerk insisted on more specific information, however, so Tom added that they both had the same birthday, and that he was four times as old as Betty was when he was three times as old as Betty was when he was twice as old as Betty was. At this the clerk fainted, whereupon the young couple snatched up the license, hurried off to the preacher's, and lived happily ever after. When the clerk came to and realized that he would have to complete his records some way or other he began to do a little figuring, and before long had found out how old the two were.

*Can you tell too?*

# 77

Four explorers once set out afoot into a desolate and barren desert. As far as they knew there was not a spring in all the wilderness ahead of them, hence in addition to their food and equipment they had to carry all their drinking water. Burdened thus, each man was able to pack only enough to sustain one person for ten days. If they all stayed together they could of course go no farther than a five day march into the desert and still have sufficient provisions for the return trip. If after a day or two, however, one of the men were to set aside just enough of his supplies to enable him to return safely to civilization, and then distribute the balance to his companions, these might perhaps be able to push on more than five days before being compelled to turn back. Like all true scientists these men cared little for personal glory, and each was willing to do anything that might extend the distance to which some member of the expedition could penetrate the unknown country before them. Assuming that the men made the most effective use of this spirit of self-sacrifice, and that the operations of transferring food from one pack to another and caching it, if necessary, were done only at the end of the day, and assuming also that once a man returned to civilization he did not set out again with additional supplies,

*How far into the desert was one of the men able to venture?*

# 78

With how few bearers can an explorer make a six-day march across an absolutely barren desert if he and the available bearers can each carry only enough food and water to last one man four days?

# 79

How long will it take a man to cross a barren and waterless desert one hundred miles wide if he can walk twenty miles a day but can carry only enough food and water for three days? For simplicity assume that the only places where supplies can safely be cached are at the points reached after one or more full days travel.

# 80

A party of five explorers is on one bank of a river and a party of five warriors is on the other, and each group wishes to cross to the opposite side. The only means of transportation is a dugout canoe which will hold just three persons. Only one warrior and one explorer know how to paddle. Moreover, for obvious reasons, it is unhealthy for the warriors to outnumber the explorers in the boat or on either shore.

*How is it possible for the two parties to cross the stream in safety?*

# 81

Under the conditions of the preceding problem is it possible for a group of six explorers and a group of six warriors each to pass in safety to the opposite shore?

# 82

In elementary geometry the notions of *congruent* or absolutely identical figures, and *similar* or proportional figures are of fundamental importance. At a somewhat more advanced level in pure mathematics, and in such applied fields as structural organic chemistry and electric circuit analysis, still another relation between figures has become important. This is the property of what might be called *essential similarity* or *structural identity*. It implies that two figures, though not necessarily congruent or even similar, are nonetheless constructed of the same number of elementary components, similarly connected. Thus any two normal men, though differing markedly, perhaps, in their various measurements, are structurally alike, and this structural identity is in no way affected by the relative movement of the component parts — arms, legs, fingers, etc. More abstractly, the configurations shown in Figure 1 illustrate this idea both positively and negatively.

Though each pattern is composed of five points and five line-segements, or arcs, only numbers 4, 8, and 12 are essentially the same. The others, though put together from the same components, are definitely dissimilar, each from all the rest, in the manner in which their elements are connected.

Of the many problems springing from this notion, the following is a fairly easy and typical example.

In how many essentially different ways can six islands be joined by bridges so that each island can be reached from every other island, and so that three of the islands have three bridges leading from them, two of the islands have two bridges leading from them, and one of the islands has only one bridge leading from it?

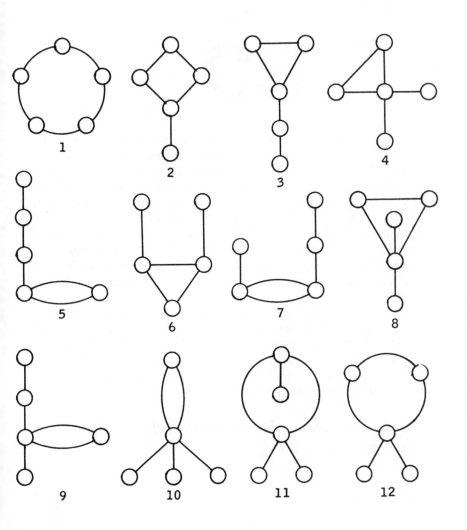

FIGURE 1.

# 83

In an old and much worn book of travels, dating from the times when a man who had journeyed beyond the hills that guarded his own village was an object of awe to his fellows, I once came upon a description of a remarkable city of the east. According to the narrator, this city was built upon ten islands connected in the following manner. Five bridges led from the islands to the mainland. Moreover four of the islands had four bridges leading from them, three of the islands had three bridges leading from them, two of the islands had two bridges leading from them, and one island could be reached by only one bridge.

No doubt in its time this description had provided many simple folk with a vicarious sense of exploration and adventure. In fact I read it with keen interest until suddenly in a moment of unwonted penetration I perceived that the whole thing was a hoax, and that no such city could exist anywhere in this or in any other world.

*What is the fallacy that stamps this description as impossible?*

# 84

To those who have successfully outgrown their early dread of arithmetic, coded computations are usually interesting and rather easy puzzles. The following multiplication in which each letter stands for a different digit is an example of this sort of problem.

```
        S O E
        U P E
        ─────
      N T R E
    O O A O
  N S H U
  ───────────
  N R R N P E
```

This can be deciphered with no further clues, but there is one too good to conceal. When the letters are arranged in the order of the numbers they represent they spell out a phrase which makes a very keen observation on the art of puzzle solving.

*For what number does each letter stand?*

# 85

When the staffs of the Gibsonville *Gazette* and the Centralia *Clarion* met for their annual baseball game at the Hillsboro County Fair it was decided by the unanimous assent of all concerned that flipping a coin or tossing up a bat to determine which side should take the field first was entirely inconsistent with the literary pretensions of the players. So it was agreed, as being more in keeping with the spirit of their profession, that all eighteen players should line up and count off alphabetically, and the first player who was 'counted' with the initial letter of his own name would choose whether his team should bat first or not. The players lined up and the captain of the Clarion team began. However fate seemed vexed at the impudence of the players in rejecting the time-honored device of the coin, and refused to give them a decision. The counting went steadily on

$$... a, b, c, ... x, y, z, a, b, ... x, y, z, a, b, ...$$

again and again, still no one called out his own initial. Finally after at least a score of turns through the alphabet they gave up and decided to toss a quarter after all. Unfortunately the quarter got lost in the grass, and before it could be found a storm came up and the game was postponed until the following year. Thus there was no box-score to be published, and the make-up of each team remained shrouded in mystery. From devious sources, however, it leaked out that the total group of eighteen players included

| | | |
|---|---|---|
| Adams | Randolph | Carver |
| Miller | Gerson | Babcock |
| Taylor | Brown | Jenkins |
| Smith | Lucas | Morton |
| Sawyer | Timmons | Young |
| Flynn | Myers | Peters |

*Who played for each team?*

# 86

In spite of appearances the following is not a spelling lesson but a multiplication problem in which each digit has been replaced by a different letter.

```
      F U R
      D O G
     -------
      A G E R
    D R I P
    F U R
   ----------
    R I P E R
```

*What two numbers were multiplied?*

# 87

Many merchants adopt the policy of marking their price tags in a code in which each digit from zero to nine is represented by a different letter. This enables the salesmen to tell at a glance the price of an article and at the same time keeps the customers in ignorance of the cost until the clerks reveal it.

So habitual was this practice with a certain Mr. Pythagoras J. Countinghouse that he began to do all his calculations with letters instead of with numbers, to the great discomfiture of his bookkeepers. Such a system is much too simple to remain long a secret, however, and one day a customer found a scrap of paper in the store with the following computation on it, and in almost no time at all had figured out just which letter stood for each number.

```
E C A ) F D B H J ( A B J
        C G G
        ─────
        A G A H
        A A E A
        ─────
          K D D J
          K D B H
          ─────
            A J
```

*Can you too decode this long division?*

# 88

It's an old saying that "two wrongs don't make a right."
However here is one case where the proverb is not quite true.
For although it is undeniably correct to say that in the two
subtractions

$$
\begin{array}{r}
N\ I\ N\ E \\
-\ T\ E\ N \\
\hline
T\ W\ O
\end{array}
\qquad\qquad
\begin{array}{r}
N\ I\ N\ E \\
-\ O\ N\ E \\
\hline
A\ L\ L
\end{array}
$$

we have two wrongs, nevertheless when the digits which the
various letters represent are correctly identified the two calculations will be found to be absolutely right.

*What number must each letter represent in order that
these two subtractions may simultaneously be decoded
into correct computations?*

# 89

Things are not always what they seem. What is true from one point of view may be false from another and vice versa, and here is a puzzle to prove it. Despite the fact that every arithmetic teacher in the land would unhesitatingly declare that it is incorrect to write

$$
\begin{array}{r}
S\ E\ V\ E\ N \\
-\ N\ I\ N\ E \\
\hline
E\ I\ G\ H\ T
\end{array}
$$

it is nonetheless true that as a puzzle in which each letter represents a different digit it is correct subtraction, and in fact can be successfully decoded in two quite different ways.

*What digits do the various letters stand for in each of the two possible solutions?*

# 90

The last puzzle was in sense paradoxical, for although at first glance it appeared to be obviously wrong it proved to be right. Here is one of the opposite character:

$$
\begin{array}{r}
E\ L\ E\ V\ E\ N \\
-\ T\ H\ R\ E\ E \\
\hline
E\ I\ G\ H\ T
\end{array}
$$

On the face of it this seems to be entirely and indisputably correct, but if we regard it as a coded subtraction in which each letter represents a different digit it simply cannot be deciphered.

*How can this be proved?*

# 91

For purposes of reassurance after the last two problems, here is one which is incorrect both as an exercise in arithmetic and as a puzzle.

$$
\begin{array}{r}
S\ E\ V\ E\ N \\
+\ N\ I\ N\ E \\
\hline
E\ I\ G\ H\ T
\end{array}
$$

*What is the reason that this simple addition cannot be decoded?*

# 92

One of the most discouraging things in life these days is the fact that from the individual household right up to the national government it seems impossible to practice economy successfully. To do so certainly requires a lot of figuring, and the following puzzle shows why even careful figuring isn't enough.

At the basis of all attempts to economize is the calculation

$$
\begin{array}{r}
S\ P\ E\ N\ D \\
-L\ E\ S\ S \\
\hline
M\ O\ N\ E\ Y
\end{array}
$$

and at least as a puzzle in which each letter represents a different digit it is not merely hard, it is absolutely impossible.

*Can you devise a proof that this subtraction cannot be decoded?*

# 93

In the following example of multiplication most of the digits have been suppressed and replaced by dots. Those that remain are not necessarily all of the 4's, 5's, and 6's in the example.

```
      6 . .
      . . .
    ─────────
      . . .
    . . . .
  . 5 . 5
  ─────────────
  . . 5 . 4 .
```

*Can you restore the suppressed digits?*

# 94

Only a few of the digits in this long division have been retained, the rest have been indiscriminately replaced by dots.

```
. . ) . . . . . ( . . 8
      . . 1
      ─────
       . .
       . .
      ─────
      . 8 .
      . . .
      ─────
      4 2
```

*Can you determine the missing digits and complete the calculation?*

# 95

Supply the missing digits in the following long division.

```
. 4 . ) . 9 8 . . . ( . . .
        . 7 . .
        ───────
        . . 4 .
        . 7 . .
        ───────
        3 . . .
        . . . .
        ───────
```

# 96

The incomplete multiplication problem

```
            . 7 .
            . 6 .
          ─────────
          . . 3 .
          . . 6 .
        3 . . .
        ─────────
        . 1 . . 1 .
```

is probably easier than most to finish because more digits have been left than are actually needed in the reconstruction. It is therefore interesting to determine how much of the given skeleton can be eliminated and still leave the problem with a unique solution. Actually there are two distinct ways in which the seven given digits can be reduced to six with the property that the problem can be uniquely reconstructed from them.

*Can you find the superfluous digits?*

# 97

Like the last puzzle, this one also contains more information than is actually required for the reconstruction.

```
          . . . 3
          . 4 .
        ─────────
        1 . . 1 .
        . . . 9 .
        . . . 6 .
        ─────────
        . 4 . . 8 . .
```

In fact there are exactly three digits, among those given, any one of which can be omitted without destroying the uniqueness of the required reconstruction.

*Which are they?*

# 98

In a certain problem in multiplication one of the digits was replaced on each occurrence by the letter X, another digit was replaced on each occurrence by the letter Y, and the remaining digits were completely suppressed, yielding

$$
\begin{array}{r}
\cdot\ \cdot\ \cdot \\
\text{X}\ \cdot \\
\hline
\text{X}\ \cdot\ \cdot\ \text{Y} \\
\cdot\ \text{X}\ \text{Y} \\
\hline
\cdot\ \text{Y}\ \text{X}\ \text{Y}
\end{array}
$$

*What two numbers were multiplied?*

# 99

In a certain .multiplication problem if one of the digits is replaced throughout by the letter X and all other digits are left completely unspecified, the result is

```
      . X X .
        . . .
      _____
      . . X . .
      . . . . X
    X . . . X
    _____
    . . . . . . .
```

*What two numbers were multiplied?*

# 100

In a certain problem in long division if the odd digits are all replaced by the letter O and the even digits are all replaced by the letter E the result is

```
O O E ) E E O O E ( O O E
        E O E
        ‾‾‾‾‾
        O O O
        O E E
        ‾‾‾‾‾
          E O E
          E O E
          ‾‾‾‾‾
```

*Can you decode the computation?*

# 101

If the letter A represents equally well any of the digits 0, 1, 2, 3, or 4, and if, similarly, the letter Z stands for any of the digits 5, 6, 7, 8, or 9, decode the following multiplication.

```
        A Z A
        A A Z
        ‾‾‾‾‾
      A A A A
    A A Z Z
    Z A A
    ‾‾‾‾‾‾‾‾‾
    Z A Z A A
```

# SOLUTIONS

# SOLUTIONS

1. Brown is the manager, Jones the teller, and Smith the cashier.

2. Clark is the carpenter, Daw the painter, and Fuller the plumber.

3. The party announced the engagements of Dorothy to Jim, Jean to Tom, and Virginia to Bill.

4. Carter is the grocer, Flynn the banker, Milne the druggist, and Savage the architect.

5. Brown is the accountant, Clark the president, Jones the manager, and Smith the cashier.

6. Clark is the druggist, Jones the grocer, Morgan the butcher, and Smith the policeman.

7. Brown is the architect, Clark the lawyer, Jones the doctor, and Smith the banker.

8. Miss Ames, Miss Brown, Conroy, Davis, and Evans hold respectively the positions of manager, cashier, floorwalker, buyer, and clerk.

9. Allen, Bennett, Clark, Davis, and Ewing are respectively the manager, the clerk, the floorwalker, the cashier, and the buyer.

10. The last names of Jane, Janice, Jack, Jasper, and Jim are Cramer, Carter, Clark, Clayton, and Carver, respectively.

11. Mr. Smith is the teacher, Mrs. Smith the lawyer, their son the postmaster, Mr. Smith's sister the grocer, and Mrs. Smith's father the preacher.

12. Mrs. Arthur, Miss Bascomb, Mrs. Conroy, Duval, Eggleston, and Furness teach French, Latin, mathematics, English, history, and economics, respectively.

13. Clayton was the policeman, Forbes the murderer, Graham the witness, Holgate the victim, McFee the judge, and Warren the hangman.

14. Bill is married to Mary, Ed is married to Helen, and Tom is married to Grace. Bill shot 98 and Tom shot 96.

# Solutions

15. Miss Ainsley is the secretary of Yates, the lawyer; Miss Barnette is Dr. Vernon's secretary; and Miss Coulter is the secretary of Wilson, the architect.

16. Art is the brakeman, John the conductor, Pete the engineer, and Tom the fireman. Pete and Tom are brothers. John is Tom's son and Pete's nephew.

17. Alice, Betty, Carol and Dorothy are married to George, Harry, Frank, and Ed, respectively, and were dancing with Frank, Ed, Harry, and George, respectively.

18. Mrs. Abbott had to go to the hardware store, Mrs. Briggs had to go to the bank, Mrs. Culver had to go to the grocery store, and Mrs. Denny had to go to the shoe store.

19. Allen, the architect, has his office on the eighth floor; Brady, the lawyer, has his office on the third floor; McCoy, the dentist, has his office on the fifth floor; and Smith, the accountant, has his office on the fifteenth floor.

20. Adams, the poet, was reading a play; Brown, the historian, was reading a novel; Clark, the novelist, was reading poetry; and Davis, the playwright, was reading history.

21. Brown.

22. Alice is the oldest, then Carl, then Bill.

23. Tom is the oldest, then Jack, then Howard.

24. Dick caught the most, followed in order by Tom, Jack, and Al.

25. Tom was the strongest, followed in order by Hank, Bill, and Joe.

26. Jennings was the best golfer, followed in order by Crawford, Bowman, and Stewart.

27. Grace and Helen were playing against Alice and Mary. Grace was the oldest, followed in order by Helen, Mary, and Alice.

28. Sixty-eight.

**29.** Of the 78 who drink coffee, 78—48=30 do not drink tea. Of the 71 who drink tea, 71—48=23 do not drink coffee. The three non-overlappng classes of individuals, those who drink coffee alone (30), those who drink tea alone (23), and those who drink both (48), total 101. But the reporter gave the number of consumers interviewed as 100. It was this inaccuracy which cost him his job.

**30.** Since there are no childless couples every family must have at least one girl, either as an only child or as the sister (required by the second fact) of such boys as there may be. Thus there must be at least as many girls as families. But then, since there are more boys than girls, the total number of children must necessarily be more than twice the number of families, that is, more than the total number of adults since there are just two adults per family. This contradicts the first fact of the report and constitutes the inconsistency for which the census taker was reprimanded.

**31.** Ten.

**32.** There were three families, one with a single boy, one with two girls and a boy, and one with two girls and three boys.

**33.** Margaret Marshall went to the bank and to the grocery store, Doris Price went to the bank and to the hardware store, Ethel Torrey went to the butcher shop and the grocery store, and so did Lucille Winters.

**34.** Mitchell teaches French and history, Morgan teaches biology and English, and Myers teaches economics and mathematics.

**35.** Jacob spoke German and Italian, John spoke French and Italian, Peter spoke English and French, and William spoke English and Italian.

**36.** There were six men representing four lodges.

**37.** There were ten men representing five fraternities.

**38.** Norris Atwood, Martin Bartlett, Louis Campbell, Peter Donovan, and Oliver Easterling. Atwood would speak to

Bartlett, Donovan, and Easterling; Bartlett would speak to Atwood and Easterling; Campbell would speak only to Donovan; Donovan would speak to Atwood, Campbell, and Easterling; and Easterling would speak to Atwood, Bartlett, and Donovan.

39. Colter must be president, Blaine must be vice-president, and Ebert must be secretary.

40. Flynn for president, Ewald for vice-president, Congreve for secretary, and Burton for treasurer.

41. The committee must consist of Davis, French, Grant, and Hughes.

42. Jones and Smith but not Brown.

43. A  B  C  D
    Y  X  W  Z

44. Louise and Allan Barber, Dorothy and Henry Cutler, Beth and Victor Drake.

45. Lewis is the clerk, Miller is the cashier, and Nelson is the accountant.

46. No.

47. The God of Diplomacy was on the left, the God of Falsehood was in the middle, and the God of Truth was on the right.

48. Jack, Jean, Lucy, and Paul received B, A, D, and C, respectively.

49. a. Gus.  b. Dave.

50. Grace was twenty-three, Helen was twenty-five, and Mary was twenty-two.

51. Brown was the average citizen, Jones the criminal, and Smith the Judge. Brown was the guilty party.

52. O'Neil was the murderer.

53. Ames, Brown, Miss Clark, and Miss Davis teach chemistry, Latin, history, and mathematics, respectively.

**54.** George and Virginia are the father and mother. Howard and Dorothy are the children.

**55.** Brown is the teacher, Jones the policeman, and Smith the fireman.

**56.** Ed was the winner, followed by Jim, Bill, and Tom, in that order.

**57.** Joe.

**58.** Ed is taking biology, chemistry, and history; Howard is taking biology, chemistry, and mathematics; John is taking biology, history, and mathematics.

**59.** Bill caught seven, Jack caught ten, and Tom caught nine.

**60.** Margaret Adams, Patricia Bates, Dorothy Clark, and Jean Douglas.

**61.** Brown is the tennis player, Fairgrieve the golfer, Leonard the bowler, and Whittier the fisherman.

**62.** Dick Brown, Bill Harris, Carl Jones, and Al Smith.

**63.** Bill was the younger boy, John the older. The interview took place on Tuesday.

**64.** In every case the contents of each drawer can be inferred by drawing once from the drawer marked **One Black-One White.**

**65.** Red.

**66.** The king could not have left fewer than three black marks for then the men bearing such marks would have seen more white marks than black and remained seated. Moreover, if the king had marked just three of the men with black spots then when all arose, one of the three bearing such marks would surely have concluded at once that he had such a mark, for the contrary supposition would prove that there were fewer than three black marks in which case, as pointed out above, not all of the men would have arisen. Since no one was able thus to identify his mark without delay, the king must have marked each man with a black spot.

## Solutions

The man who finally decided that his mark was black was clever enough to extend this reasoning one step further. If he supposed that his mark was white, then surely one of the other three men would have reasoned, as outlined above, that he (the third man) had a black mark. Since none of the three had reached a conclusion but still stood silent, the problem must have been more baffling, that is he must have had a black mark and not a white one.

67. The only combination of boxes and contents for which the first two men could easily infer the color of their third ball while the third man could not is the following:

| Box | 1 | 2 | 3 | 4 |
|---|---|---|---|---|
| Label | B B W | B W W | B B B | W W W |
| Contents | B B B | B B W | W W W | B W W |

Reasoning to this conclusion, the blind man correctly identified the contents of each box.

68. Mary Davis, Helen Jones, and Dorothy Smith.

69. Jack Conner, Tom Mogran, Al Smith, and Bill Wells.

70. Selling the melons at five for 50 cents, which was essentially what John did, would be correct only if each group of five consisted of three of the cheap melons and two of the more expensive ones. But since there were just as many melons of each kind to begin with, by selling three of the cheap ones for each pair of the more expensive ones, the former would be sold out sooner than the latter, after which further sales at 10 cents apiece could be made only by selling the more expensive melons at a $2\frac{1}{2}$ cents loss. To have a total loss of $1.00 resulting from a loss of $2\frac{1}{2}$ cents per melon, 40 of the more expensive melons must have been sold after the cheaper ones were gone. This means that originally there must have been 120 melons of each kind, since only two-thirds of the expensive melons would have been sold when the supply of the cheaper ones was exhausted, and the remaining third then constituted the 40 melons that were sold at a loss.

71. Three miles per hour.

**72.** When the Pleasure City was going upstream her actual speed was

 normal, or still water speed minus speed of current

and when she was returning downstream her actual speed was

 normal, or still water speed plus speed of current

In either case the jar containing the jewels floated downstream with speed equal to the speed of the current. Hence when the jar and the ship were separating (before the ship turned back, that is) the distance between them was increasing at a rate equal to

 (normal speed minus speed of current) plus speed of current or just

    normal speed

Likewise, after the ship put about and began to overtake the jar the distance between them diminished at a rate equal to

 (normal speed plus speed of current) minus speed of current

or again just

    normal speed

Thus the speed of separation and the speed of overtaking were the same, and hence, the time of separation must have been equal to the time of overtaking. From the given data the time of overtaking was 2:45 minus 1:30 or one hour and fifteen minutes. Counting back this interval from 1:30, when the ship put about, gives 12:15 as the time when the jar was thrown into the water. The afternoon maid was the only one of the three suspects whose whereabouts were not definitely known at this time. Hence only she could have thrown the jar into the river, and so she must have been the thief.

**73.** The passenger train is three times as fast as the freight train.

**74.** The fish was sixteen strokes away.

**75.** Bert Smith is eight, David Allen is seven, Arthur Allen is four, and Carl Smith is two.

## Solutions

**76.** Tom was twenty-four and Betty was twenty-one.

**77.** One of the men was able to go a distance equal to a ten-day march. (If it is possible to transfer and cache food anywhere, then by making suitable transfers and caches $\dfrac{5}{4}, \dfrac{35}{12}$, and $\dfrac{65}{12}$ days marches from their starting point one of the men can penetrate the desert to a distance equal to $10 \dfrac{5}{12}$ days marches.)

**78.** With two bearers, one of whom turns back at the end of the first day, the other of whom turns back at the end of the second day, the explorer can cross the desert in safety.

**79.** By first caching food and water along the way, the man can cross the desert in fifteen days. (If it is possible to cache food anywhere, the man can cross the desert in $11 \dfrac{4}{5}$ days by caching suitable amounts $\dfrac{2}{5}$, 1, and 2 days marches from his starting point.)

**80.** If each warrior be represented by a dot and each explorer by a small circle, and if the individual in each group who knows how to paddle be distinguished by an underscore, then the manner in which the parties can cross the stream in safety may be indicated as follows:

**81.** No.

**82.** The islands can be joined in thirteen essentially different ways:

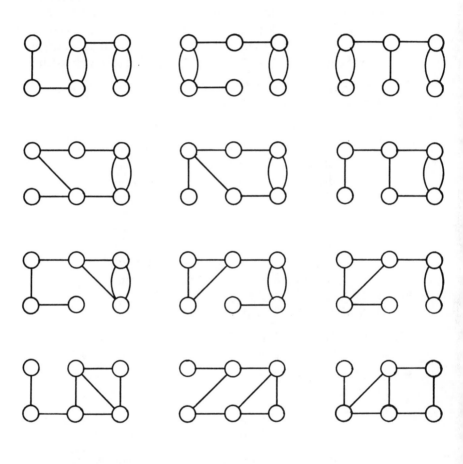

## Solutions

83. Evidently for any system of bridges there must be twice as many ends as there are bridges, that is, the number of bridge ends must be even. But according to the account given in the problem the number of bridge ends is 4×4 plus 3×3 plus 2×2 plus 1×1, plus 5 more for the ends of the bridges that reach the mainland. The total number of ends is thus 35, an odd number and hence impossible.

84. N O  S U R E  P A T H
    1 2  3 4 5 6  7 8 9 0

85.

| Clarion | Gazette |
|---------|---------|
| Babcock | Adams |
| Brown | Carver |
| Flynn | Gerson |
| Jenkins | Miller |
| Lucas | Myers |
| Peters | Morton |
| Randolph | Smith |
| Taylor | Sawyer |
| Timmons | Young |

86. 1 2 3 4 5 6 7 8 9 0
    D A F O R E G I U P

87. A B C D E F G H J K
    2 6 7 8 3 9 4 0 5 1

88. N W I A T O E L
    1 2 3 5 6 8 9 0

89. 1 2 3 4 5 6 7 8  or  1 2 3 4 5 6 7 8
    E S T N V I H G  or  V T G E S N I H

90. Since the answer contains no digit in the extreme left column, it is apparent that E equals 1. From the second column from the right it is also evident that H must be either 0 (zero) or 9. If H equals 9, then in the first column on the right N must equal 0 and T must be 9, which is impossible since H already represents 9 and two letters cannot stand for the same number. On the other hand, if H equals 0 a contradiction also arises for then in the fourth column from the right I must be either 0 or 1,

which is impossible since these numbers are represented by H and E respectively. Thus the problem is impossible of solution.

**91.** In three different columns E and N are added together, each time with a different result. This is impossible since only two different totals can arise, depending on whether 0 or 1 is carried over from the column on the right.

**92.** In the third column, E from E must leave either 0 or 9, depending upon whether or not 1 must be borrowed from this column to carry out the subtraction in the preceding column. But if N is 9, as it is in the case when 1 is borrowed, the upper number in the preceding column (being 9) is so large that no borrowing would be necessary. On the other hand, if N is 0, which will be the case only if there is no borrowing for the preceding subtraction, then the upper number in the preceding column, being 0 would inevitably require borrowing no matter what the subtracted number S might be. Thus, each of the only two possibilities for N leads to a contradiction, and so the problem is impossible of solution.

**93.**

```
            6 4 5
            7 2 1
          ---------
            6 4 5
        1 2 9 0
      4 5 1 5
      -----------
      4 6 5 0 4 5
```

**94.**

```
      4 3 ) 3 0 9 1 6 ( 7 1 8
            3 0 1
            -------
              8 1
              4 3
              -----
              3 8 6
              3 4 4
              -------
                4 2
```

## Solutions

**95.**  3 4 7 ) 2 9 8 0 7 3 ) 8 5 9
 2 7 7 6
 ─────────
  2 0 4 7
  1 7 3 5
  ─────────
   3 1 2 3
   3 1 2 3

**96.**      4 7 8
          8 6 3
         ─────────
        1 4 3 4
      2 8 6 8
    3 8 2 4
    ─────────────
    4 1 2 5 1 4

Either the 7 in the first line or the 6 in the fourth line from the top is superfluous, for when either of these is omitted the problem can still be uniquely reconstructed.

**97.**      4 4 7 3
            5 4 3
         ─────────
        1 3 4 1 9
      1 7 8 9 2
    2 2 3 6 5
    ─────────────
    2 4 2 8 8 3 9

If any one of the following digits is omitted the problem can still be uniquely reconstructed: The 3 in the first line, the 4 in the second line, the 1 at the left end of the third line.

**98.**      3 6 4
            2 7
         ─────────
        2 5 4 8
      7 2 8
    ─────────
    9 8 2 8

**99.**      8 6 6 2
            8 3 4
         ─────────
        3 4 6 4 8
      2 5 9 8 6
    6 9 2 9 6
    ─────────────
    7 2 2 4 1 0 8

**100.**

```
1 1 6 ) 8 4 9 1 2 ( 7 3 2
        8 1 2
        ─────
          3 7 1
          3 4 8
          ─────
            2 3 2
            2 3 2
            ─────
```

**101.**

```
            3 7 2
            2 4 6
          ─────
        2 2 3 2
    1 4 8 8
    7 4 4
    ─────────
    9 1 5 1 2
```

# A CATALOG OF SELECTED DOVER
# BOOKS IN ALL FIELDS OF INTEREST

CONCERNING THE SPIRITUAL IN ART, Wassily Kandinsky. Pioneering work by father of abstract art. Thoughts on color theory, nature of art. Analysis of earlier masters. 12 illustrations. 80pp. of text. 5⅜ x 8½. 23411-8

ANIMALS: 1,419 Copyright-Free Illustrations of Mammals, Birds, Fish, Insects, etc., Jim Harter (ed.). Clear wood engravings present, in extremely lifelike poses, over 1,000 species of animals. One of the most extensive pictorial sourcebooks of its kind. Captions. Index. 284pp. 9 x 12. 23766-4

CELTIC ART: The Methods of Construction, George Bain. Simple geometric techniques for making Celtic interlacements, spirals, Kells-type initials, animals, humans, etc. Over 500 illustrations. 160pp. 9 x 12. (Available in U.S. only.) 22923-8

AN ATLAS OF ANATOMY FOR ARTISTS, Fritz Schider. Most thorough reference work on art anatomy in the world. Hundreds of illustrations, including selections from works by Vesalius, Leonardo, Goya, Ingres, Michelangelo, others. 593 illustrations. 192pp. 7⅛ x 10¼. 20241-0

CELTIC HAND STROKE-BY-STROKE (Irish Half-Uncial from "The Book of Kells"): An Arthur Baker Calligraphy Manual, Arthur Baker. Complete guide to creating each letter of the alphabet in distinctive Celtic manner. Covers hand position, strokes, pens, inks, paper, more. Illustrated. 48pp. 8¼ x 11. 24336-2

EASY ORIGAMI, John Montroll. Charming collection of 32 projects (hat, cup, pelican, piano, swan, many more) specially designed for the novice origami hobbyist. Clearly illustrated easy-to-follow instructions insure that even beginning papercrafters will achieve successful results. 48pp. 8¼ x 11. 27298-2

THE COMPLETE BOOK OF BIRDHOUSE CONSTRUCTION FOR WOOD-WORKERS, Scott D. Campbell. Detailed instructions, illustrations, tables. Also data on bird habitat and instinct patterns. Bibliography. 3 tables. 63 illustrations in 15 figures. 48pp. 5¼ x 8½. 24407-5

BLOOMINGDALE'S ILLUSTRATED 1886 CATALOG: Fashions, Dry Goods and Housewares, Bloomingdale Brothers. Famed merchants' extremely rare catalog depicting about 1,700 products: clothing, housewares, firearms, dry goods, jewelry, more. Invaluable for dating, identifying vintage items. Also, copyright-free graphics for artists, designers. Co-published with Henry Ford Museum & Greenfield Village. 160pp. 8¼ x 11. 25780-0

HISTORIC COSTUME IN PICTURES, Braun & Schneider. Over 1,450 costumed figures in clearly detailed engravings–from dawn of civilization to end of 19th century. Captions. Many folk costumes. 256pp. 8⅜ x 11¾. 23150-X

# CATALOG OF DOVER BOOKS

STICKLEY CRAFTSMAN FURNITURE CATALOGS, Gustav Stickley and L. & J. G. Stickley. Beautiful, functional furniture in two authentic catalogs from 1910. 594 illustrations, including 277 photos, show settles, rockers, armchairs, reclining chairs, bookcases, desks, tables. 183pp. 6½ x 9¼.                          23838-5

AMERICAN LOCOMOTIVES IN HISTORIC PHOTOGRAPHS: 1858 to 1949, Ron Ziel (ed.). A rare collection of 126 meticulously detailed official photographs, called "builder portraits," of American locomotives that majestically chronicle the rise of steam locomotive power in America. Introduction. Detailed captions. xi+ 129pp. 9 x 12.                          27393-8

AMERICA'S LIGHTHOUSES: An Illustrated History, Francis Ross Holland, Jr. Delightfully written, profusely illustrated fact-filled survey of over 200 American lighthouses since 1716. History, anecdotes, technological advances, more. 240pp. 8 x 10¾.                          25576-X

TOWARDS A NEW ARCHITECTURE, Le Corbusier. Pioneering manifesto by founder of "International School." Technical and aesthetic theories, views of industry, economics, relation of form to function, "mass-production split" and much more. Profusely illustrated. 320pp. 6⅛ x 9¼. (Available in U.S. only.)                          25023-7

HOW THE OTHER HALF LIVES, Jacob Riis. Famous journalistic record, exposing poverty and degradation of New York slums around 1900, by major social reformer. 100 striking and influential photographs. 233pp. 10 x 7⅞.                          22012-5

FRUIT KEY AND TWIG KEY TO TREES AND SHRUBS, William M. Harlow. One of the handiest and most widely used identification aids. Fruit key covers 120 deciduous and evergreen species; twig key 160 deciduous species. Easily used. Over 300 photographs. 126pp. 5⅜ x 8½.                          20511-8

COMMON BIRD SONGS, Dr. Donald J. Borror. Songs of 60 most common U.S. birds: robins, sparrows, cardinals, bluejays, finches, more—arranged in order of increasing complexity. Up to 9 variations of songs of each species.
Cassette and manual 99911-4

ORCHIDS AS HOUSE PLANTS, Rebecca Tyson Northen. Grow cattleyas and many other kinds of orchids—in a window, in a case, or under artificial light. 63 illustrations. 148pp. 5⅜ x 8½.                          23261-1

MONSTER MAZES, Dave Phillips. Masterful mazes at four levels of difficulty. Avoid deadly perils and evil creatures to find magical treasures. Solutions for all 32 exciting illustrated puzzles. 48pp. 8¼ x 11.                          26005-4

MOZART'S DON GIOVANNI (DOVER OPERA LIBRETTO SERIES), Wolfgang Amadeus Mozart. Introduced and translated by Ellen H. Bleiler. Standard Italian libretto, with complete English translation. Convenient and thoroughly portable—an ideal companion for reading along with a recording or the performance itself. Introduction. List of characters. Plot summary. 121pp. 5¼ x 8½.                          24944-1

TECHNICAL MANUAL AND DICTIONARY OF CLASSICAL BALLET, Gail Grant. Defines, explains, comments on steps, movements, poses and concepts. 15-page pictorial section. Basic book for student, viewer. 127pp. 5⅜ x 8½.                          21843-0

THE CLARINET AND CLARINET PLAYING, David Pino. Lively, comprehensive work features suggestions about technique, musicianship, and musical interpretation, as well as guidelines for teaching, making your own reeds, and preparing for public performance. Includes an intriguing look at clarinet history. "A godsend," *The Clarinet,* Journal of the International Clarinet Society. Appendixes. 7 illus. 320pp. 5⅜ x 8½. 40270-3

HOLLYWOOD GLAMOR PORTRAITS, John Kobal (ed.). 145 photos from 1926-49. Harlow, Gable, Bogart, Bacall; 94 stars in all. Full background on photographers, technical aspects. 160pp. 8⅜ x 11¼. 23352-9

THE ANNOTATED CASEY AT THE BAT: A Collection of Ballads about the Mighty Casey/Third, Revised Edition, Martin Gardner (ed.). Amusing sequels and parodies of one of America's best-loved poems: Casey's Revenge, Why Casey Whiffed, Casey's Sister at the Bat, others. 256pp. 5⅜ x 8½. 28598-7

THE RAVEN AND OTHER FAVORITE POEMS, Edgar Allan Poe. Over 40 of the author's most memorable poems: "The Bells," "Ulalume," "Israfel," "To Helen," "The Conqueror Worm," "Eldorado," "Annabel Lee," many more. Alphabetic lists of titles and first lines. 64pp. 5$\frac{3}{16}$ x 8¼. 26685-0

PERSONAL MEMOIRS OF U. S. GRANT, Ulysses Simpson Grant. Intelligent, deeply moving firsthand account of Civil War campaigns, considered by many the finest military memoirs ever written. Includes letters, historic photographs, maps and more. 528pp. 6⅛ x 9¼. 28587-1

ANCIENT EGYPTIAN MATERIALS AND INDUSTRIES, A. Lucas and J. Harris. Fascinating, comprehensive, thoroughly documented text describes this ancient civilization's vast resources and the processes that incorporated them in daily life, including the use of animal products, building materials, cosmetics, perfumes and incense, fibers, glazed ware, glass and its manufacture, materials used in the mummification process, and much more. 544pp. 6⅛ x 9¼. (Available in U.S. only.) 40446-3

RUSSIAN STORIES/RUSSKIE RASSKAZY: A Dual-Language Book, edited by Gleb Struve. Twelve tales by such masters as Chekhov, Tolstoy, Dostoevsky, Pushkin, others. Excellent word-for-word English translations on facing pages, plus teaching and study aids, Russian/English vocabulary, biographical/critical introductions, more. 416pp. 5⅜ x 8½. 26244-8

PHILADELPHIA THEN AND NOW: 60 Sites Photographed in the Past and Present, Kenneth Finkel and Susan Oyama. Rare photographs of City Hall, Logan Square, Independence Hall, Betsy Ross House, other landmarks juxtaposed with contemporary views. Captures changing face of historic city. Introduction. Captions. 128pp. 8¼ x 11. 25790-8

AIA ARCHITECTURAL GUIDE TO NASSAU AND SUFFOLK COUNTIES, LONG ISLAND, The American Institute of Architects, Long Island Chapter, and the Society for the Preservation of Long Island Antiquities. Comprehensive, well-researched and generously illustrated volume brings to life over three centuries of Long Island's great architectural heritage. More than 240 photographs with authoritative, extensively detailed captions. 176pp. 8¼ x 11. 26946-9

NORTH AMERICAN INDIAN LIFE: Customs and Traditions of 23 Tribes, Elsie Clews Parsons (ed.). 27 fictionalized essays by noted anthropologists examine religion, customs, government, additional facets of life among the Winnebago, Crow, Zuni, Eskimo, other tribes. 480pp. 6⅛ x 9¼. 27377-6

# CATALOG OF DOVER BOOKS

FRANK LLOYD WRIGHT'S DANA HOUSE, Donald Hoffmann. Pictorial essay of residential masterpiece with over 160 interior and exterior photos, plans, elevations, sketches and studies. 128pp. 9¼ x 10¾.                                      29120-0

THE MALE AND FEMALE FIGURE IN MOTION: 60 Classic Photographic Sequences, Eadweard Muybridge. 60 true-action photographs of men and women walking, running, climbing, bending, turning, etc., reproduced from rare 19th-century masterpiece. vi + 121pp. 9 x 12.                                      24745-7

1001 QUESTIONS ANSWERED ABOUT THE SEASHORE, N. J. Berrill and Jacquelyn Berrill. Queries answered about dolphins, sea snails, sponges, starfish, fishes, shore birds, many others. Covers appearance, breeding, growth, feeding, much more. 305pp. 5¼ x 8¼.                                      23366-9

ATTRACTING BIRDS TO YOUR YARD, William J. Weber. Easy-to-follow guide offers advice on how to attract the greatest diversity of birds: birdhouses, feeders, water and waterers, much more. 96pp. 5³⁄₁₆ x 8¼.                                      28927-3

MEDICINAL AND OTHER USES OF NORTH AMERICAN PLANTS: A Historical Survey with Special Reference to the Eastern Indian Tribes, Charlotte Erichsen-Brown. Chronological historical citations document 500 years of usage of plants, trees, shrubs native to eastern Canada, northeastern U.S. Also complete identifying information. 343 illustrations. 544pp. 6½ x 9¼.                                      25951-X

STORYBOOK MAZES, Dave Phillips. 23 stories and mazes on two-page spreads: Wizard of Oz, Treasure Island, Robin Hood, etc. Solutions. 64pp. 8¼ x 11.    23628-5

AMERICAN NEGRO SONGS: 230 Folk Songs and Spirituals, Religious and Secular, John W. Work. This authoritative study traces the African influences of songs sung and played by black Americans at work, in church, and as entertainment. The author discusses the lyric significance of such songs as "Swing Low, Sweet Chariot," "John Henry," and others and offers the words and music for 230 songs. Bibliography. Index of Song Titles. 272pp. 6½ x 9¼.                                      40271-1

MOVIE-STAR PORTRAITS OF THE FORTIES, John Kobal (ed.). 163 glamor, studio photos of 106 stars of the 1940s: Rita Hayworth, Ava Gardner, Marlon Brando, Clark Gable, many more. 176pp. 8⅜ x 11¼.                                      23546-7

BENCHLEY LOST AND FOUND, Robert Benchley. Finest humor from early 30s, about pet peeves, child psychologists, post office and others. Mostly unavailable elsewhere. 73 illustrations by Peter Arno and others. 183pp. 5⅜ x 8½.                                      22410-4

YEKL and THE IMPORTED BRIDEGROOM AND OTHER STORIES OF YIDDISH NEW YORK, Abraham Cahan. Film Hester Street based on *Yekl* (1896). Novel, other stories among first about Jewish immigrants on N.Y.'s East Side. 240pp. 5⅜ x 8½.                                      22427-9

SELECTED POEMS, Walt Whitman. Generous sampling from *Leaves of Grass*. Twenty-four poems include "I Hear America Singing," "Song of the Open Road," "I Sing the Body Electric," "When Lilacs Last in the Dooryard Bloom'd," "O Captain! My Captain!"–all reprinted from an authoritative edition. Lists of titles and first lines. 128pp. 5³⁄₁₆ x 8¼.                                      26878-0

# CATALOG OF DOVER BOOKS

THE BEST TALES OF HOFFMANN, E. T. A. Hoffmann. 10 of Hoffmann's most important stories: "Nutcracker and the King of Mice," "The Golden Flowerpot," etc. 458pp. 5⅜ x 8½. 21793-0

FROM FETISH TO GOD IN ANCIENT EGYPT, E. A. Wallis Budge. Rich detailed survey of Egyptian conception of "God" and gods, magic, cult of animals, Osiris, more. Also, superb English translations of hymns and legends. 240 illustrations. 545pp. 5⅜ x 8½. 25803-3

FRENCH STORIES/CONTES FRANÇAIS: A Dual-Language Book, Wallace Fowlie. Ten stories by French masters, Voltaire to Camus: "Micromegas" by Voltaire; "The Atheist's Mass" by Balzac; "Minuet" by de Maupassant; "The Guest" by Camus, six more. Excellent English translations on facing pages. Also French-English vocabulary list, exercises, more. 352pp. 5⅜ x 8½. 26443-2

CHICAGO AT THE TURN OF THE CENTURY IN PHOTOGRAPHS: 122 Historic Views from the Collections of the Chicago Historical Society, Larry A. Viskochil. Rare large-format prints offer detailed views of City Hall, State Street, the Loop, Hull House, Union Station, many other landmarks, circa 1904-1913. Introduction. Captions. Maps. 144pp. 9⅜ x 12¼. 24656-6

OLD BROOKLYN IN EARLY PHOTOGRAPHS, 1865-1929, William Lee Younger. Luna Park, Gravesend race track, construction of Grand Army Plaza, moving of Hotel Brighton, etc. 157 previously unpublished photographs. 165pp. 8⅞ x 11¾. 23587-4

THE MYTHS OF THE NORTH AMERICAN INDIANS, Lewis Spence. Rich anthology of the myths and legends of the Algonquins, Iroquois, Pawnees and Sioux, prefaced by an extensive historical and ethnological commentary. 36 illustrations. 480pp. 5⅜ x 8½. 25967-6

AN ENCYCLOPEDIA OF BATTLES: Accounts of Over 1,560 Battles from 1479 B.C. to the Present, David Eggenberger. Essential details of every major battle in recorded history from the first battle of Megiddo in 1479 B.C. to Grenada in 1984. List of Battle Maps. New Appendix covering the years 1967-1984. Index. 99 illustrations. 544pp. 6½ x 9¼. 24913-1

SAILING ALONE AROUND THE WORLD, Captain Joshua Slocum. First man to sail around the world, alone, in small boat. One of great feats of seamanship told in delightful manner. 67 illustrations. 294pp. 5⅜ x 8½. 20326-3

ANARCHISM AND OTHER ESSAYS, Emma Goldman. Powerful, penetrating, prophetic essays on direct action, role of minorities, prison reform, puritan hypocrisy, violence, etc. 271pp. 5⅜ x 8½. 22484-8

MYTHS OF THE HINDUS AND BUDDHISTS, Ananda K. Coomaraswamy and Sister Nivedita. Great stories of the epics; deeds of Krishna, Shiva, taken from puranas, Vedas, folk tales; etc. 32 illustrations. 400pp. 5⅜ x 8½. 21759-0

THE TRAUMA OF BIRTH, Otto Rank. Rank's controversial thesis that anxiety neurosis is caused by profound psychological trauma which occurs at birth. 256pp. 5⅜ x 8½. 27974-X

A THEOLOGICO-POLITICAL TREATISE, Benedict Spinoza. Also contains unfinished Political Treatise. Great classic on religious liberty, theory of government on common consent. R. Elwes translation. Total of 421pp. 5⅜ x 8½. 20249-6

# CATALOG OF DOVER BOOKS

MY BONDAGE AND MY FREEDOM, Frederick Douglass. Born a slave, Douglass became outspoken force in antislavery movement. The best of Douglass' autobiographies. Graphic description of slave life. 464pp. 5⅜ x 8½.          22457-0

FOLLOWING THE EQUATOR: A Journey Around the World, Mark Twain. Fascinating humorous account of 1897 voyage to Hawaii, Australia, India, New Zealand, etc. Ironic, bemused reports on peoples, customs, climate, flora and fauna, politics, much more. 197 illustrations. 720pp. 5⅜ x 8½.          26113-1

THE PEOPLE CALLED SHAKERS, Edward D. Andrews. Definitive study of Shakers: origins, beliefs, practices, dances, social organization, furniture and crafts, etc. 33 illustrations. 351pp. 5⅜ x 8½.          21081-2

THE MYTHS OF GREECE AND ROME, H. A. Guerber. A classic of mythology, generously illustrated, long prized for its simple, graphic, accurate retelling of the principal myths of Greece and Rome, and for its commentary on their origins and significance. With 64 illustrations by Michelangelo, Raphael, Titian, Rubens, Canova, Bernini and others. 480pp. 5⅜ x 8½.          27584-1

PSYCHOLOGY OF MUSIC, Carl E. Seashore. Classic work discusses music as a medium from psychological viewpoint. Clear treatment of physical acoustics, auditory apparatus, sound perception, development of musical skills, nature of musical feeling, host of other topics. 88 figures. 408pp. 5⅜ x 8½.          21851-1

THE PHILOSOPHY OF HISTORY, Georg W. Hegel. Great classic of Western thought develops concept that history is not chance but rational process, the evolution of freedom. 457pp. 5⅜ x 8½.          20112-0

THE BOOK OF TEA, Kakuzo Okakura. Minor classic of the Orient: entertaining, charming explanation, interpretation of traditional Japanese culture in terms of tea ceremony. 94pp. 5⅜ x 8½.          20070-1

LIFE IN ANCIENT EGYPT, Adolf Erman. Fullest, most thorough, detailed older account with much not in more recent books, domestic life, religion, magic, medicine, commerce, much more. Many illustrations reproduce tomb paintings, carvings, hieroglyphs, etc. 597pp. 5⅜ x 8½.          22632-8

SUNDIALS, Their Theory and Construction, Albert Waugh. Far and away the best, most thorough coverage of ideas, mathematics concerned, types, construction, adjusting anywhere. Simple, nontechnical treatment allows even children to build several of these dials. Over 100 illustrations. 230pp. 5⅜ x 8½.          22947-5

THEORETICAL HYDRODYNAMICS, L. M. Milne-Thomson. Classic exposition of the mathematical theory of fluid motion, applicable to both hydrodynamics and aerodynamics. Over 600 exercises. 768pp. 6⅛ x 9¼.          68970-0

SONGS OF EXPERIENCE: Facsimile Reproduction with 26 Plates in Full Color, William Blake. 26 full-color plates from a rare 1826 edition. Includes "The Tyger," "London," "Holy Thursday," and other poems. Printed text of poems. 48pp. 5¼ x 7.          24636-1

OLD-TIME VIGNETTES IN FULL COLOR, Carol Belanger Grafton (ed.). Over 390 charming, often sentimental illustrations, selected from archives of Victorian graphics—pretty women posing, children playing, food, flowers, kittens and puppies, smiling cherubs, birds and butterflies, much more. All copyright-free. 48pp. 9¼ x 12¼.          27269-9

# CATALOG OF DOVER BOOKS

PERSPECTIVE FOR ARTISTS, Rex Vicat Cole. Depth, perspective of sky and sea, shadows, much more, not usually covered. 391 diagrams, 81 reproductions of drawings and paintings. 279pp. 5⅜ x 8½. 22487-2

DRAWING THE LIVING FIGURE, Joseph Sheppard. Innovative approach to artistic anatomy focuses on specifics of surface anatomy, rather than muscles and bones. Over 170 drawings of live models in front, back and side views, and in widely varying poses. Accompanying diagrams. 177 illustrations. Introduction. Index. 144pp. 8⅜ x11¼. 26723-7

GOTHIC AND OLD ENGLISH ALPHABETS: 100 Complete Fonts, Dan X. Solo. Add power, elegance to posters, signs, other graphics with 100 stunning copyright-free alphabets: Blackstone, Dolbey, Germania, 97 more—including many lower-case, numerals, punctuation marks. 104pp. 8⅛ x 11. 24695-7

HOW TO DO BEADWORK, Mary White. Fundamental book on craft from simple projects to five-bead chains and woven works. 106 illustrations. 142pp. 5⅜ x 8. 20697-1

THE BOOK OF WOOD CARVING, Charles Marshall Sayers. Finest book for beginners discusses fundamentals and offers 34 designs. "Absolutely first rate . . . well thought out and well executed."–E. J. Tangerman. 118pp. 7¾ x 10⅝. 23654-4

ILLUSTRATED CATALOG OF CIVIL WAR MILITARY GOODS: Union Army Weapons, Insignia, Uniform Accessories, and Other Equipment, Schuyler, Hartley, and Graham. Rare, profusely illustrated 1846 catalog includes Union Army uniform and dress regulations, arms and ammunition, coats, insignia, flags, swords, rifles, etc. 226 illustrations. 160pp. 9 x 12. 24939-5

WOMEN'S FASHIONS OF THE EARLY 1900s: An Unabridged Republication of "New York Fashions, 1909," National Cloak & Suit Co. Rare catalog of mail-order fashions documents women's and children's clothing styles shortly after the turn of the century. Captions offer full descriptions, prices. Invaluable resource for fashion, costume historians. Approximately 725 illustrations. 128pp. 8⅜ x 11¼. 27276-1

THE 1912 AND 1915 GUSTAV STICKLEY FURNITURE CATALOGS, Gustav Stickley. With over 200 detailed illustrations and descriptions, these two catalogs are essential reading and reference materials and identification guides for Stickley furniture. Captions cite materials, dimensions and prices. 112pp. 6½ x 9¼. 26676-1

EARLY AMERICAN LOCOMOTIVES, John H. White, Jr. Finest locomotive engravings from early 19th century: historical (1804–74), main-line (after 1870), special, foreign, etc. 147 plates. 142pp. 11⅜ x 8¼. 22772-3

THE TALL SHIPS OF TODAY IN PHOTOGRAPHS, Frank O. Braynard. Lavishly illustrated tribute to nearly 100 majestic contemporary sailing vessels: Amerigo Vespucci, Clearwater, Constitution, Eagle, Mayflower, Sea Cloud, Victory, many more. Authoritative captions provide statistics, background on each ship. 190 black-and-white photographs and illustrations. Introduction. 128pp. 8⅞ x 11¾. 27163-3

LITTLE BOOK OF EARLY AMERICAN CRAFTS AND TRADES, Peter Stockham (ed.). 1807 children's book explains crafts and trades: baker, hatter, cooper, potter, and many others. 23 copperplate illustrations. 140pp. 4⅝ x 6. 23336-7

VICTORIAN FASHIONS AND COSTUMES FROM HARPER'S BAZAR, 1867–1898, Stella Blum (ed.). Day costumes, evening wear, sports clothes, shoes, hats, other accessories in over 1,000 detailed engravings. 320pp. 9⅜ x 12¼. 22990-4

GUSTAV STICKLEY, THE CRAFTSMAN, Mary Ann Smith. Superb study surveys broad scope of Stickley's achievement, especially in architecture. Design philosophy, rise and fall of the Craftsman empire, descriptions and floor plans for many Craftsman houses, more. 86 black-and-white halftones. 31 line illustrations. Introduction 208pp. 6½ x 9¼. 27210-9

THE LONG ISLAND RAIL ROAD IN EARLY PHOTOGRAPHS, Ron Ziel. Over 220 rare photos, informative text document origin ( 1844) and development of rail service on Long Island. Vintage views of early trains, locomotives, stations, passengers, crews, much more. Captions. 8⅞ x 11¾. 26301-0

VOYAGE OF THE LIBERDADE, Joshua Slocum. Great 19th-century mariner's thrilling, first-hand account of the wreck of his ship off South America, the 35-foot boat he built from the wreckage, and its remarkable voyage home. 128pp. 5⅜ x 8½. 40022-0

TEN BOOKS ON ARCHITECTURE, Vitruvius. The most important book ever written on architecture. Early Roman aesthetics, technology, classical orders, site selection, all other aspects. Morgan translation. 331pp. 5⅜ x 8½. 20645-9

THE HUMAN FIGURE IN MOTION, Eadweard Muybridge. More than 4,500 stopped-action photos, in action series, showing undraped men, women, children jumping, lying down, throwing, sitting, wrestling, carrying, etc. 390pp. 7⅞ x 10⅝. 20204-6 Clothbd.

TREES OF THE EASTERN AND CENTRAL UNITED STATES AND CANADA, William M. Harlow. Best one-volume guide to 140 trees. Full descriptions, woodlore, range, etc. Over 600 illustrations. Handy size. 288pp. 4½ x 6⅜. 20395-6

SONGS OF WESTERN BIRDS, Dr. Donald J. Borror. Complete song and call repertoire of 60 western species, including flycatchers, juncoes, cactus wrens, many more—includes fully illustrated booklet. Cassette and manual 99913-0

GROWING AND USING HERBS AND SPICES, Milo Miloradovich. Versatile handbook provides all the information needed for cultivation and use of all the herbs and spices available in North America. 4 illustrations. Index. Glossary. 236pp. 5⅜ x 8½. 25058-X

BIG BOOK OF MAZES AND LABYRINTHS, Walter Shepherd. 50 mazes and labyrinths in all—classical, solid, ripple, and more—in one great volume. Perfect inexpensive puzzler for clever youngsters. Full solutions. 112pp. 8⅛ x 11. 22951-3

# CATALOG OF DOVER BOOKS

PIANO TUNING, J. Cree Fischer. Clearest, best book for beginner, amateur. Simple repairs, raising dropped notes, tuning by easy method of flattened fifths. No previous skills needed. 4 illustrations. 201pp. 5⅜ x 8½.                     23267-0

HINTS TO SINGERS, Lillian Nordica. Selecting the right teacher, developing confidence, overcoming stage fright, and many other important skills receive thoughtful discussion in this indispensible guide, written by a world-famous diva of four decades' experience. 96pp. 5⅜ x 8½.                     40094-8

THE COMPLETE NONSENSE OF EDWARD LEAR, Edward Lear. All nonsense limericks, zany alphabets, Owl and Pussycat, songs, nonsense botany, etc., illustrated by Lear. Total of 320pp. 5⅜ x 8½. (Available in U.S. only.)                     20167-8

VICTORIAN PARLOUR POETRY: An Annotated Anthology, Michael R. Turner. 117 gems by Longfellow, Tennyson, Browning, many lesser-known poets. "The Village Blacksmith," "Curfew Must Not Ring Tonight," "Only a Baby Small," dozens more, often difficult to find elsewhere. Index of poets, titles, first lines. xxiii + 325pp. 5⅜ x 8¼.                     27044-0

DUBLINERS, James Joyce. Fifteen stories offer vivid, tightly focused observations of the lives of Dublin's poorer classes. At least one, "The Dead," is considered a masterpiece. Reprinted complete and unabridged from standard edition. 160pp. 5³⁄₁₆ x 8¼.                     26870-5

GREAT WEIRD TALES: 14 Stories by Lovecraft, Blackwood, Machen and Others, S. T. Joshi (ed.). 14 spellbinding tales, including "The Sin Eater," by Fiona McLeod, "The Eye Above the Mantel," by Frank Belknap Long, as well as renowned works by R. H. Barlow, Lord Dunsany, Arthur Machen, W. C. Morrow and eight other masters of the genre. 256pp. 5⅜ x 8½. (Available in U.S. only.)                     40436-6

THE BOOK OF THE SACRED MAGIC OF ABRAMELIN THE MAGE, translated by S. MacGregor Mathers. Medieval manuscript of ceremonial magic. Basic document in Aleister Crowley, Golden Dawn groups. 268pp. 5⅜ x 8½.     23211-5

NEW RUSSIAN-ENGLISH AND ENGLISH-RUSSIAN DICTIONARY, M. A. O'Brien. This is a remarkably handy Russian dictionary, containing a surprising amount of information, including over 70,000 entries. 366pp. 4½ x 6⅛.     20208-9

HISTORIC HOMES OF THE AMERICAN PRESIDENTS, Second, Revised Edition, Irvin Haas. A traveler's guide to American Presidential homes, most open to the public, depicting and describing homes occupied by every American President from George Washington to George Bush. With visiting hours, admission charges, travel routes. 175 photographs. Index. 160pp. 8¼ x 11.                     26751-2

NEW YORK IN THE FORTIES, Andreas Feininger. 162 brilliant photographs by the well-known photographer, formerly with *Life* magazine. Commuters, shoppers, Times Square at night, much else from city at its peak. Captions by John von Hartz. 181pp. 9¼ x 10¾.                     23585-8

INDIAN SIGN LANGUAGE, William Tomkins. Over 525 signs developed by Sioux and other tribes. Written instructions and diagrams. Also 290 pictographs. 111pp. 6⅛ x 9¼.                     22029-X

# CATALOG OF DOVER BOOKS

ANATOMY: A Complete Guide for Artists, Joseph Sheppard. A master of figure drawing shows artists how to render human anatomy convincingly. Over 460 illustrations. 224pp. 8⅜ x 11¼. 27279-6

MEDIEVAL CALLIGRAPHY: Its History and Technique, Marc Drogin. Spirited history, comprehensive instruction manual covers 13 styles (ca. 4th century through 15th). Excellent photographs; directions for duplicating medieval techniques with modern tools. 224pp. 8⅜ x 11¼. 26142-5

DRIED FLOWERS: How to Prepare Them, Sarah Whitlock and Martha Rankin. Complete instructions on how to use silica gel, meal and borax, perlite aggregate, sand and borax, glycerine and water to create attractive permanent flower arrangements. 12 illustrations. 32pp. 5⅜ x 8½. 21802-3

EASY-TO-MAKE BIRD FEEDERS FOR WOODWORKERS, Scott D. Campbell. Detailed, simple-to-use guide for designing, constructing, caring for and using feeders. Text, illustrations for 12 classic and contemporary designs. 96pp. 5⅜ x 8½. 25847-5

SCOTTISH WONDER TALES FROM MYTH AND LEGEND, Donald A. Mackenzie. 16 lively tales tell of giants rumbling down mountainsides, of a magic wand that turns stone pillars into warriors, of gods and goddesses, evil hags, powerful forces and more. 240pp. 5⅜ x 8½. 29677-6

THE HISTORY OF UNDERCLOTHES, C. Willett Cunnington and Phyllis Cunnington. Fascinating, well-documented survey covering six centuries of English undergarments, enhanced with over 100 illustrations: 12th-century laced-up bodice, footed long drawers (1795), 19th-century bustles, 19th-century corsets for men, Victorian "bust improvers," much more. 272pp. 5⅜ x 8¼. 27124-2

ARTS AND CRAFTS FURNITURE: The Complete Brooks Catalog of 1912, Brooks Manufacturing Co. Photos and detailed descriptions of more than 150 now very collectible furniture designs from the Arts and Crafts movement depict davenports, settees, buffets, desks, tables, chairs, bedsteads, dressers and more, all built of solid, quarter-sawed oak. Invaluable for students and enthusiasts of antiques, Americana and the decorative arts. 80pp. 6½ x 9¼. 27471-3

WILBUR AND ORVILLE: A Biography of the Wright Brothers, Fred Howard. Definitive, crisply written study tells the full story of the brothers' lives and work. A vividly written biography, unparalleled in scope and color, that also captures the spirit of an extraordinary era. 560pp. 6⅛ x 9¼. 40297-5

THE ARTS OF THE SAILOR: Knotting, Splicing and Ropework, Hervey Garrett Smith. Indispensable shipboard reference covers tools, basic knots and useful hitches; handsewing and canvas work, more. Over 100 illustrations. Delightful reading for sea lovers. 256pp. 5⅜ x 8½. 26440-8

FRANK LLOYD WRIGHT'S FALLINGWATER: The House and Its History, Second, Revised Edition, Donald Hoffmann. A total revision–both in text and illustrations–of the standard document on Fallingwater, the boldest, most personal architectural statement of Wright's mature years, updated with valuable new material from the recently opened Frank Lloyd Wright Archives. "Fascinating"–*The New York Times*. 116 illustrations. 128pp. 9¼ x 10¾. 27430-6

# CATALOG OF DOVER BOOKS

PHOTOGRAPHIC SKETCHBOOK OF THE CIVIL WAR, Alexander Gardner. 100 photos taken on field during the Civil War. Famous shots of Manassas Harper's Ferry, Lincoln, Richmond, slave pens, etc. 244pp. 10⅝ x 8¼. 22731-6

FIVE ACRES AND INDEPENDENCE, Maurice G. Kains. Great back-to-the-land classic explains basics of self-sufficient farming. The one book to get. 95 illustrations. 397pp. 5⅜ x 8½. 20974-1

SONGS OF EASTERN BIRDS, Dr. Donald J. Borror. Songs and calls of 60 species most common to eastern U.S.: warblers, woodpeckers, flycatchers, thrushes, larks, many more in high-quality recording. Cassette and manual 99912-2

A MODERN HERBAL, Margaret Grieve. Much the fullest, most exact, most useful compilation of herbal material. Gigantic alphabetical encyclopedia, from aconite to zedoary, gives botanical information, medical properties, folklore, economic uses, much else. Indispensable to serious reader. 161 illustrations. 888pp. 6½ x 9¼. 2-vol. set. (Available in U.S. only.) Vol. I: 22798-7
Vol. II: 22799-5

HIDDEN TREASURE MAZE BOOK, Dave Phillips. Solve 34 challenging mazes accompanied by heroic tales of adventure. Evil dragons, people-eating plants, bloodthirsty giants, many more dangerous adversaries lurk at every twist and turn. 34 mazes, stories, solutions. 48pp. 8¼ x 11. 24566-7

LETTERS OF W. A. MOZART, Wolfgang A. Mozart. Remarkable letters show bawdy wit, humor, imagination, musical insights, contemporary musical world; includes some letters from Leopold Mozart. 276pp. 5⅜ x 8½. 22859-2

BASIC PRINCIPLES OF CLASSICAL BALLET, Agrippina Vaganova. Great Russian theoretician, teacher explains methods for teaching classical ballet. 118 illustrations. 175pp. 5⅜ x 8½. 22036-2

THE JUMPING FROG, Mark Twain. Revenge edition. The original story of The Celebrated Jumping Frog of Calaveras County, a hapless French translation, and Twain's hilarious "retranslation" from the French. 12 illustrations. 66pp. 5⅜ x 8½. 22686-7

BEST REMEMBERED POEMS, Martin Gardner (ed.). The 126 poems in this superb collection of 19th- and 20th-century British and American verse range from Shelley's "To a Skylark" to the impassioned "Renascence" of Edna St. Vincent Millay and to Edward Lear's whimsical "The Owl and the Pussycat." 224pp. 5⅜ x 8½. 27165-X

COMPLETE SONNETS, William Shakespeare. Over 150 exquisite poems deal with love, friendship, the tyranny of time, beauty's evanescence, death and other themes in language of remarkable power, precision and beauty. Glossary of archaic terms. 80pp. 5³⁄₁₆ x 8¼. 26686-9

THE BATTLES THAT CHANGED HISTORY, Fletcher Pratt. Eminent historian profiles 16 crucial conflicts, ancient to modern, that changed the course of civilization. 352pp. 5⅜ x 8½. 41129-X

THE WIT AND HUMOR OF OSCAR WILDE, Alvin Redman (ed.). More than 1,000 ripostes, paradoxes, wisecracks: Work is the curse of the drinking classes; I can resist everything except temptation; etc. 258pp. 5⅜ x 8½. 20602-5

SHAKESPEARE LEXICON AND QUOTATION DICTIONARY, Alexander Schmidt. Full definitions, locations, shades of meaning in every word in plays and poems. More than 50,000 exact quotations. 1,485pp. 6½ x 9¼. 2-vol. set.
Vol. 1: 22726-X
Vol. 2: 22727-8

SELECTED POEMS, Emily Dickinson. Over 100 best-known, best-loved poems by one of America's foremost poets, reprinted from authoritative early editions. No comparable edition at this price. Index of first lines. 64pp. 5³⁄₁₆ x 8¼. 26466-1

THE INSIDIOUS DR. FU-MANCHU, Sax Rohmer. The first of the popular mystery series introduces a pair of English detectives to their archnemesis, the diabolical Dr. Fu-Manchu. Flavorful atmosphere, fast-paced action, and colorful characters enliven this classic of the genre. 208pp. 5³⁄₁₆ x 8¼. 29898-1

THE MALLEUS MALEFICARUM OF KRAMER AND SPRENGER, translated by Montague Summers. Full text of most important witchhunter's "bible," used by both Catholics and Protestants. 278pp. 6⅝ x 10. 22802-9

SPANISH STORIES/CUENTOS ESPAÑOLES: A Dual-Language Book, Angel Flores (ed.). Unique format offers 13 great stories in Spanish by Cervantes, Borges, others. Faithful English translations on facing pages. 352pp. 5⅜ x 8½. 25399-6

GARDEN CITY, LONG ISLAND, IN EARLY PHOTOGRAPHS, 1869–1919, Mildred H. Smith. Handsome treasury of 118 vintage pictures, accompanied by carefully researched captions, document the Garden City Hotel fire (1899), the Vanderbilt Cup Race (1908), the first airmail flight departing from the Nassau Boulevard Aerodrome (1911), and much more. 96pp. 8⅞ x 11¾. 40669-5

OLD QUEENS, N.Y., IN EARLY PHOTOGRAPHS, Vincent F. Seyfried and William Asadorian. Over 160 rare photographs of Maspeth, Jamaica, Jackson Heights, and other areas. Vintage views of DeWitt Clinton mansion, 1939 World's Fair and more. Captions. 192pp. 8⅞ x 11. 26358-4

CAPTURED BY THE INDIANS: 15 Firsthand Accounts, 1750-1870, Frederick Drimmer. Astounding true historical accounts of grisly torture, bloody conflicts, relentless pursuits, miraculous escapes and more, by people who lived to tell the tale. 384pp. 5⅜ x 8½. 24901-8

THE WORLD'S GREAT SPEECHES (Fourth Enlarged Edition), Lewis Copeland, Lawrence W. Lamm, and Stephen J. McKenna. Nearly 300 speeches provide public speakers with a wealth of updated quotes and inspiration–from Pericles' funeral oration and William Jennings Bryan's "Cross of Gold Speech" to Malcolm X's powerful words on the Black Revolution and Earl of Spenser's tribute to his sister, Diana, Princess of Wales. 944pp. 5⅜ x 8⅜. 40903-1

THE BOOK OF THE SWORD, Sir Richard F. Burton. Great Victorian scholar/adventurer's eloquent, erudite history of the "queen of weapons"–from prehistory to early Roman Empire. Evolution and development of early swords, variations (sabre, broadsword, cutlass, scimitar, etc.), much more. 336pp. 6⅛ x 9¼. 25434-8

CATALOG OF DOVER BOOKS

AUTOBIOGRAPHY: The Story of My Experiments with Truth, Mohandas K. Gandhi. Boyhood, legal studies, purification, the growth of the Satyagraha (nonviolent protest) movement. Critical, inspiring work of the man responsible for the freedom of India. 480pp. 5⅜ x 8½. (Available in U.S. only.)                          24593-4

CELTIC MYTHS AND LEGENDS, T. W. Rolleston. Masterful retelling of Irish and Welsh stories and tales. Cuchulain, King Arthur, Deirdre, the Grail, many more. First paperback edition. 58 full-page illustrations. 512pp. 5⅜ x 8½.                          26507-2

THE PRINCIPLES OF PSYCHOLOGY, William James. Famous long course complete, unabridged. Stream of thought, time perception, memory, experimental methods; great work decades ahead of its time. 94 figures. 1,391pp. 5⅜ x 8½. 2-vol. set.
Vol. I: 20381-6   Vol. II: 20382-4

THE WORLD AS WILL AND REPRESENTATION, Arthur Schopenhauer. Definitive English translation of Schopenhauer's life work, correcting more than 1,000 errors, omissions in earlier translations. Translated by E. F. J. Payne. Total of 1,269pp. 5⅜ x 8½. 2-vol. set.              Vol. 1: 21761-2   Vol. 2: 21762-0

MAGIC AND MYSTERY IN TIBET, Madame Alexandra David-Neel. Experiences among lamas, magicians, sages, sorcerers, Bonpa wizards. A true psychic discovery. 32 illustrations. 321pp. 5⅜ x 8½. (Available in U.S. only.)                          22682-4

THE EGYPTIAN BOOK OF THE DEAD, E. A. Wallis Budge. Complete reproduction of Ani's papyrus, finest ever found. Full hieroglyphic text, interlinear transliteration, word-for-word translation, smooth translation. 533pp. 6½ x 9¼.       21866-X

MATHEMATICS FOR THE NONMATHEMATICIAN, Morris Kline. Detailed, college-level treatment of mathematics in cultural and historical context, with numerous exercises. Recommended Reading Lists. Tables. Numerous figures. 641pp. 5⅜ x 8½.
24823-2

PROBABILISTIC METHODS IN THE THEORY OF STRUCTURES, Isaac Elishakoff. Well-written introduction covers the elements of the theory of probability from two or more random variables, the reliability of such multivariable structures, the theory of random function, Monte Carlo methods of treating problems incapable of exact solution, and more. Examples. 502pp. 5⅜ x 8½.                          40691-1

THE RIME OF THE ANCIENT MARINER, Gustave Doré, S. T. Coleridge. Doré's finest work; 34 plates capture moods, subtleties of poem. Flawless full-size reproductions printed on facing pages with authoritative text of poem. "Beautiful. Simply beautiful."—Publisher's Weekly. 77pp. 9¼ x 12.                          22305-1

NORTH AMERICAN INDIAN DESIGNS FOR ARTISTS AND CRAFTSPEOPLE, Eva Wilson. Over 360 authentic copyright-free designs adapted from Navajo blankets, Hopi pottery, Sioux buffalo hides, more. Geometrics, symbolic figures, plant and animal motifs, etc. 128pp. 8⅜ x 11. (Not for sale in the United Kingdom.)            25341-4

SCULPTURE: Principles and Practice, Louis Slobodkin. Step-by-step approach to clay, plaster, metals, stone; classical and modern. 253 drawings, photos. 255pp. 8⅛ x 11.
22960-2

THE INFLUENCE OF SEA POWER UPON HISTORY, 1660–1783, A. T. Mahan. Influential classic of naval history and tactics still used as text in war colleges. First paperback edition. 4 maps. 24 battle plans. 640pp. 5⅜ x 8½.                          25509-3

*CATALOG OF DOVER BOOKS*

THE STORY OF THE TITANIC AS TOLD BY ITS SURVIVORS, Jack Winocour (ed.). What it was really like. Panic, despair, shocking inefficiency, and a little heroism. More thrilling than any fictional account. 26 illustrations. 320pp. 5⅜ x 8½. 20610-6

FAIRY AND FOLK TALES OF THE IRISH PEASANTRY, William Butler Yeats (ed.). Treasury of 64 tales from the twilight world of Celtic myth and legend: "The Soul Cages," "The Kildare Pooka," "King O'Toole and his Goose," many more. Introduction and Notes by W. B. Yeats. 352pp. 5⅜ x 8½. 26941-8

BUDDHIST MAHAYANA TEXTS, E. B. Cowell and others (eds.). Superb, accurate translations of basic documents in Mahayana Buddhism, highly important in history of religions. The Buddha-karita of Asvaghosha, Larger Sukhavativyuha, more. 448pp. 5⅜ x 8½. 25552-2

ONE TWO THREE . . . INFINITY: Facts and Speculations of Science, George Gamow. Great physicist's fascinating, readable overview of contemporary science: number theory, relativity, fourth dimension, entropy, genes, atomic structure, much more. 128 illustrations. Index. 352pp. 5⅜ x 8½. 25664-2

EXPERIMENTATION AND MEASUREMENT, W. J. Youden. Introductory manual explains laws of measurement in simple terms and offers tips for achieving accuracy and minimizing errors. Mathematics of measurement, use of instruments, experimenting with machines. 1994 edition. Foreword. Preface. Introduction. Epilogue. Selected Readings. Glossary. Index. Tables and figures. 128pp. 5⅜ x 8½. 40451-X

DALÍ ON MODERN ART: The Cuckolds of Antiquated Modern Art, Salvador Dalí. Influential painter skewers modern art and its practitioners. Outrageous evaluations of Picasso, Cézanne, Turner, more. 15 renderings of paintings discussed. 44 calligraphic decorations by Dalí. 96pp. 5⅜ x 8½. (Available in U.S. only.) 29220-7

ANTIQUE PLAYING CARDS: A Pictorial History, Henry René D'Allemagne. Over 900 elaborate, decorative images from rare playing cards (14th–20th centuries): Bacchus, death, dancing dogs, hunting scenes, royal coats of arms, players cheating, much more. 96pp. 9¼ x 12¼. 29265-7

MAKING FURNITURE MASTERPIECES: 30 Projects with Measured Drawings, Franklin H. Gottshall. Step-by-step instructions, illustrations for constructing handsome, useful pieces, among them a Sheraton desk, Chippendale chair, Spanish desk, Queen Anne table and a William and Mary dressing mirror. 224pp. 8⅛ x 11¼. 29338-6

THE FOSSIL BOOK: A Record of Prehistoric Life, Patricia V. Rich et al. Profusely illustrated definitive guide covers everything from single-celled organisms and dinosaurs to birds and mammals and the interplay between climate and man. Over 1,500 illustrations. 760pp. 7½ x 10⅛. 29371-8

Paperbound unless otherwise indicated. Available at your book dealer, online at **www.doverpublications.com**, or by writing to Dept. GI, Dover Publications, Inc., 31 East 2nd Street, Mineola, NY 11501. For current price information or for free catalogues (please indicate field of interest), write to Dover Publications or log on to **www.doverpublications.com** and see every Dover book in print. Dover publishes more than 500 books each year on science, elementary and advanced mathematics, biology, music, art, literary history, social sciences, and other areas.